The One Percenter

Published by OurSoftspot.com

675 Biltmore Avenue- Suite G

Asheville, NC 28803

United States of America

Printing by Quinn Essentials Books & Printing, Inc.

Petaluma, CA

Cover Design and Layout: Tim Kirby

Art Work: Berszan Arus

ISBN: 978-1-7349273-0-6

(Psychology)

Copyright: © 2020 - Carl Mumpower, Ph.D.

For more information about this publication ~

www.TheOnePercenter.com

Praise for The One Percenter

"Not all of us are white kittens. Have you ever yearned to
help that very special and talented family member, student, or friend whose
life every so often inexplicably sputters and stalls? This book has
real answers."

– EDUCATOR

"Wow – it was about me. I feel like I am reading about myself, my sister, my
husband, my friends. I am wanting to know more."

– IRENE

"One of the biggest helps came from learning the reasons behind my pain
and insecurities were not from inadequacy, but complexity. The author
explains this and offers gentle advice on
how to carry that weight."

– DAVID

"I had always felt less capable than other students in school, even when I
succeeded. I now understand that much of my "fear, doubt, and insecurity"
was due to my deeper potentials – not my limits."

–ANONYMOUS

"This book helped me to understand that I am not alone, and
given me the power to move forward with my life.
Thank you – your guidance is invaluable."

– JOE

Table of Contents

Special Thanks

It took forty-three years and countless hours with many special people to complete this book. It could not have been written without a core insight that developed slowly but surely out of those contacts. My patients have taught me that my profession has blank spots.

I have met so many unique, complex, and able people who were misunderstood, overlooked or sometimes abused by a system truly wanting to help. Those who refused to surrender have been an irreplaceable source of inspiration. Thanks is due to every face and voice – those remembered and those regrettably lost in time – who made me smarter.

Much gratitude is due to Susan Kingshill and Carole Spence for their stellar editorial assistance. Both are reminders of the importance of our educators.

Two very special One Percenters – Kristianna Bartow and Rocky Beach – merit a big dose of thanks. Their smart, studied, and special angle of view made this book so much better than I could have made it on my own.

The hand of my peerless assistant, Pam Stewart, was invaluable to this effort. Tim Kirby's graciousness and talent were evident in his cover creation and other wonderful touches. Similarly, I am grateful to Berszán Árus Bence for lending his artistic hand and patience to this project.

Appreciation is also due to One Percenters David, Alex, Keith, Abby, Jordan, Anthony, Joey, Clay, Camryn, Gracie, Tim, Vickie, Isaiah, Patrick, Shane, Joanna, and Adam. Their refusal to yield to their hurdles, and press forward to their fuller potentials, merits my greatest respect.

Many thanks to my departed friend, colleague, and mentor, Don Boone, for his patience and love. Without his gifts, it is doubtful the chain of experience leading to this book would have been completed.

So much more than appreciation is due to my wife Lisa, my children Kristen and Matt, and my sisters Linda and Kimberly for their help and love. We never really do anything without the touch of others – especially our family.

I also give thanks to my parents, community, culture, and country for a bridge to my Christian faith. It remains an irreplaceable compass.

Then there are those who are pressing on through their pain in the search for solid answers in a confusing world. It is my hope that you will find some good ones here.

Introduction

We do not live on an easy planet. Everyone struggles to find their fit. Some of us more than most. For these unique individuals, life – from their first step to their very last – is too often characterized by uncertainty, obstacles and erratic traction.

Such people are frequently branded as resistant, different, distracted, or even broken. Other descriptors as well, like lazy, troubled, or mentally ill, can find a way into that mix. Those thus targeted are far too often inaccurately framed and even condemned by these misguided labels.

Much like a burn victim quietly compelled to stretch scars, these extraordinary individuals face an existence riddled with invisible pain. It is intense and rarely noted by the comfortable.

These prodigies of nature are rare – and contrary to their social tags, they are anything but dysfunctional. In fact, in a world filled with special people, they can be the most special of all.

This book is written for the one percent who truly walk the road less traveled. Knowing that complexity is sometimes best served by simplicity, most of the pages rest on a half-dozen or so sentences. Each page can be read and digested on its own and without overexertion. This is on purpose – complex people frequently find reading a tedious and unrewarding undertaking. A page or two at a time is doable for those who prefer to learn in other ways. It is enough.

This book is respectfully dedicated to that one percent who are so gifted they are sometimes laden. The mission and my wish – to help turn that unintended burden into a much intended and astonishing blessing. . .

It Begins...

His first memory traces to age three. It was a kaleidoscope of sounds, images, and feelings involving his mother, father, and a policeman.

Such people were fathered in front of a building somewhere near Mobile. The word "JAIL" was written above the door. He was stretched between his parents. His father had his arms and shoulders. His mom had his boots. They were new black and white cowboy boots.

One came off in his mother's hand just as a police officer grabbed her. His father pulled him away and put him in the back of a car. It was a big green and white car. It smelled musty. He stood in the back and looked out the window, watching the receding image of his mom.

He remembers being scared and confused. He turned to look at his father and grandfather conversing in the front seat. They were tense but somehow seemed happy.

He didn't know what to do. He didn't understand any of it. He just looked out the dark window in the direction of his mother.

He wanted to stop and go back, but the car kept on going. . .

CHAPTER ONE

What's a One Percenter?

One Percenter [n. wn pərsntər] One percent – one part in a
hundred parts; unique; extraordinary; exceptional; special

There's a funny thing about being special – it often sounds better than it actually feels. Amidst a world that thrives on conformity, being unique – truly unique – is a challenge fraught with hazards.

When it comes to being a One Percenter, "special" usually begins as anything but special. Words like awkward, strange, impaired, pained, or difficult are much more likely to come one's way. The list of designations is long and rarely tilted toward the positive.

In the beginning, unique people are similar to newborn fawns – wobbly, uncertain and vulnerable. And much like the fawn, they need help and protection.

With persistence and support, Bambi didn't die, and he didn't remain vulnerable. Thanks to the right amount of help in the right dose, he found his special place in this world.

That's our assignment – to find or build our special place in the world. That journey begins with understanding the challenges we face and how they come about. . .

It's more difficult
than it looks...

There were no more memories until his first day in a Philadelphia public school.

It was exciting – especially when the teacher came around giving out big sheets of paper and watercolor sets. He got a brand new one.

This was his first attempt at painting, and he immediately set out to create a color that no one had ever seen before. He mixed his blues, greens, yellows, and oranges. He mixed all his colors except the black and brown. In the end, that's what he had in the middle of his paper – a disappointing blob of blackish, brownish yuck.

There was nothing he could do to fix it. Besides, he knew he was out of his depth. To his right was a blond-haired girl who had it all figured out. She had painted a house, a family, a yard, and a dog. All of them were smiling.

When the bell rang, the teacher instructed the students to roll up their watercolor painting and take it home to show their parents. He made his way quickly toward the door, where he decided to ignore the teacher's guidance. He did not want his parents to see his mess.

There was a trash container at the exit. He quietly tossed his crumpled-up picture and kept on going...

We live in a hard world.

From the day we are born until our last breath. . .

. . .we are relentlessly challenged.

<u>Every</u> one of us.

But some are challenged more.

Challenge is certain; timing is unpredictable.

Sometimes it begins at birth.

Sometimes it begins in our early childhood.

Sometimes it begins with school.

Sometimes it begins with adolescence.

Sometimes it begins when we are on our own.

But it always begins – and once it does, it never stops.

We have no choice but to learn to deal with our challenges.

"Accept hardship as a necessary discipline."

– Lailah Gifty Akita

Everyone who is alive faces challenges.

We do not face the same hurdles with the same resources.

There are three inescapable truths to life's challenges—

(1) Life was not meant to be easy.

(2) We are given tools, but we must learn to use them.

(3) This is not something we can do without help.

Though life is a team sport, not all players are the same.

"Heavy hearts, like heavy clouds in the sky, are best relieved by the letting of a little water."

– Christopher Morley

Everyone has a head, heart, hand, and spirit.

Some of us have a great mind.

Some have a deep heart.

Some have a strong hand.

Some have an unflinching spirit.

Everyone is gifted in one of these four qualities.

And one is enough to anchor us to a good life.

"Life is not easy for any of us. But what of that? We must have perseverance and above all confidence in ourselves. We must believe that we are gifted for something and that this thing must be attained."

– Marie Curie

Some people are blessed with a strong mind.

They love logic.

They love facts.

They love knowledge.

They love questions.

They love solutions.

They love thinking.

They feel safest when they use their head.

And that head can do some very special things.

"Wise thinkers prevail everywhere."

– Sophocles

Some people are blessed with a deep heart.

They care.

They sense.

They feel.

They smile.

They hurt.

They love.

Most of us know someone who struggles with a disability.

But the size of their heart is bigger than what's missing.

"Truth is ever incoherent, and when the big hearts strike together, the concussion is a little stunning."

– Herman Melville

Some people have a strong hand.

They can do almost anything.

They can build.

They can play.

They can protect.

They can provide.

They can explore.

They can prevail.

Big-handed doers keep our world turning.

"The doer alone learneth."

- Friedrich Nietzsche

Some people are gifted with a dedicated spirit.

They reach for something more.

They have a strong belief in higher authority.

They understand how important faith is.

They seek to understand God's will.

They work to follow it.

These are people who civilize the world by looking beyond just the things we can see, touch, or hear.

A dedication to the truth helps mark their path.

"I believe in Christianity as I believe that the sun has risen: not only because I see it, but because by it I see everything else."

– C.S. Lewis

Everyone is strong in one way – some in more.

Around thirty percent of us are strong in **two** ways.

Two is tougher than one.

There's more to understand, learn, and juggle.
And that comes on top of life's other challenges.

Two strengths may be better than one.

But what's good is not necessarily what's easy.

Then there's the ten percent who are strong in three.

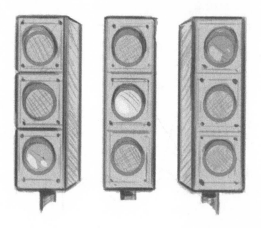

That's even tougher.

It's sort of like responding to three stoplights.

All at the same time.

With three conflicting signals, it's easy to get in a wreck.

"We are losing the ability to understand
anything that's even vaguely complex."

– Chuck Klosterman

The most challenged group are *One Percenters.*

These are the one percent who are strong in all four areas.

Balancing so many gifts can easily be overwhelming.

It's the difference between fishing with one pole or four.
We can catch more fish, or maybe just get more tangles.

Our job is to clear the tangles and catch some fish.

"Stop trying to change reality by eliminating complexity."
– David Whyte

Points of Light

Andy – *I've never really thought of myself as being complex. I just thought I was messed up. It's mostly seemed liked I was meant to be that way. I've always been clumsy, awkward, and afraid. I had no idea that there might be something good behind all that bad stuff. It's still a little strange to think about me that way. But at least it's a positive alternative to always thinking bad of myself.*

Melinda – *It's hard to totally buy into the idea that I'm different in a good way. I get the idea and really do think I'm strong in at least three of the four, but it's hard to imagine that I'm someone good when I've been feeling bad about me for so long. It's a tough change to compute! Seeing that fourth one in myself is especially tough. Could I really be smarter than I know? Someone once told me I had pretty eyes and it threw me out of sync for days. It didn't fit my view of myself. Still, it was nice to hear and try to accept something good for a change. I'm going to keep trying to do that.*

Thomas – *Wow – this explains a lot about me and my family. We are all a little strange. I thought it was mostly about some of us being screwed up, but I also thought there was genius hiding in the middle of it all. There are people in my family who have amazing moments of insight, creativity, and achievement. I like the idea that we are perhaps more special than weird. The more I think about it, the more I believe it's true. I can do something with this. I can encourage some of my siblings and nephews. I can encourage myself. I like this idea. It puts hope in front!*

Me – *Use this space to share your thoughts, feelings and reflections:*

_____
_____
_____
_____
_____
_____
_____
_____

CHAPTER TWO

The 1% Reality

Complex[n. käm-pleks] A whole made up of intricate or
interrelated parts

The problems with complexity show up quickly.

The gifted One Percenter is harder to manage, harder to
decipher, and harder to teach than individuals of a less intricate
design. That's not to say that everything is misery and woe, but
thorns are always a part of the rose.

Framing things in a positive manner is important. Early
recognition of One Percenter realities helps us do that best.
Understanding what we – and parents, teachers, and supporters
– are facing sets the stage for overcoming the challenges.

It's easier to be patient and persistent when we understand that
different does not mean broken, and that the ups and downs
have a purpose. Complexity does not find its potential without
illumination, challenge, and practice. . .

He was eight when his dad took him to Sears to buy his gold football uniform. It was all amazing. Everything was shiny and new.

The next day they drove to the YMCA. He was going to play football for the first time. It was exciting, but he was also scared. He met the coach and some of the players. No one seemed to know he did not know how to play football.

On his very first day, he found himself on the field in a line of other guys in gold uniforms. Everything next was fuzzy, like it happened in slow motion. Someone came up and pushed him and he quickly found himself on the ground. Just as suddenly, all of the running and shoving and yelling was over.

But it wasn't really over. The same thing happened again, and then again, except that after, a while no one hit him. He just stood there while everything swirled around him.

At some point, his dad and the coach yelled at him to get off the field. His dad looked dejected – even disgusted. The coach didn't look at him at all.

He sat on the bench until they went home. His dad didn't say much of anything, except "why didn't you play?"

He wanted to tell his dad that he was afraid, and that he didn't know how to play football. He had never played before. No one had taught him what to do or how to do it.

He didn't tell his dad anything. Instead, that gold uniform went under the bed. He never put it on again. He wore the shame and hurt instead.

He hid it and kept on going. . .

The problems and possibilities start early.

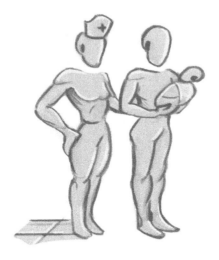

Nothing complex is easy, and easy is not always simple.

Complex things predictably take more effort to develop.

In the beginning, they are rarely at their best.

Patience is crucial.

For in that effort rests profound hope and potential.

Complex children are often difficult.

They are harder to put together. Here's why—

Human beings do not grow at the same pace.
Greater complexity equals greater breakability.
Complexity slows growth in order to nurture potential.
Growth involves pain – complexity magnifies that pain.
We have to grow up and face the world simultaneously.

Here's an important hint –

All children struggle with their limitations.

But some children struggle because of their potentials.

"The potential of the average person is like a huge ocean
unsailed, a new continent unexplored, a world of possibilities
waiting to be released and channeled toward some great good."

– Brian Tracy

Daycare and school can be tough.

Introducing a busy head, heart, mind, and spirit into the chaos of those environments can be overwhelming.

Separation anxiety,

social anxiety,

and other apprehensions can result.

Whether it be from within, without, or both—

Fear is a natural response to being overwhelmed.

Rejection, failure, and bullying are common.

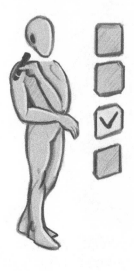

It's harder to check 4 boxes than it is 1, 2, or 3.

Complexity can trigger animosity. It can make us clumsy, inefficient, anxious, confused, hesitant, angry, shy, awkward, and a whole lot of other things that upset others.

Fighting inside and outside forces at the same time is hard.

That constant struggle can obscure our potential.

But it will more surely stimulate our growth.

"Challenge and adversity are meant to help you know who you are. Storms hit your weakness but unlock your true strength."

– Roy T. Bennet

**Sometimes we can face the opposite of rejection –
unusually generous praise and popularity.**

That's maybe better, but it is not necessarily easier.

If the rewards come too quickly and in too big a dose –
pressure, perfectionism, and performance anxiety result.

That can make it just as overwhelming as rejection.

Think of a super-talented little league ballplayer.

The constant pressure to meet their great potential can
lead to a paralyzing fear of failure.

Either extreme – rejection or validation – impairs growth.

*"So long as men praise you, you can only be sure that you are not
yet on your own true path but on someone else's."*

– Friedrich Nietzsche

One Percenters are often diagnosed with tags like ADD, depressed, oppositional, traumatized, etc.

We find comfort in labeling things we can't understand.

We find comfort in poking symptoms vs. fixing problems.

We find comfort in assuming complex things are simple.

Those pulling their pieces into a functional whole are thus easily lost in the wilderness of the mental health world.

Mental health care is more than making people behave or feel better – it's also about helping them be better.

"Our society tends to regard as a sickness any mode of thought or behavior that is inconvenient for the system. . ."

– Theodore Kaczynski

Imagine two cars.

One is a Ferrari, and the other an everyday compact.

The sedan takes about one day to build.
The Ferrari takes ninety.

The simpler the car, the faster it comes together.
The more complex, the slower it comes together.

People are like cars.
Regular people can reach their potential quickly.
Complex people take longer.

Over time, who holds the greater promise?

"The machine was so intricate, so complicated,
that he almost got dizzy looking at it. Even in its sad
state of disrepair, it was beautiful."

– Brian Selznick

Not all garden vegetables grow at the same pace.

The same is true for heads, hearts, hands, and spirits.

Uneven growth can lead to other issues like clumsiness, awkwardness, inconsistency, distractibility, insecurity, vulnerability, or hesitancy.

These are growing pains.

The more growth, the more pain.

But pain is an amazing foundation for progress.

"Growth is painful. Change is painful. But nothing is as painful as staying stuck where you do not belong."

– N.R. Narayana Murthy

A river with too much water will flood.

People are like rivers – especially complex people.

A super-active head, heart, hand, or spirit can sometimes overflow its host and create challenges.

Patience and timely aid can turn disaster into opportunity.

Still, it remains that even human floods serve a purpose.

Flooding helps clean away debris.

And we learn to swim best in deeper waters.

*"He was swimming in a sea of other people's expectations.
Men had drowned in seas like that."*

– Robert Jordan

It's easy to go from feeling different. . .

. . .to feeling abnormal, damaged, or broken.

That's a painful place to be.

That pain leads to temptations like dodging reality, taking short-cuts, and addiction to bad stuff.

These things don't work for anyone, but they really don't work for people who are more vulnerable to breaking.

The only sure way forward is to press through the pain.

"To keep our faces toward change and behave like free spirits in the presence of fate is strength undefeatable."

– Helen Keller

All things that grow are vulnerable when young.

Nurturing and protection are important.

But too much water and food can be as bad as too little.

Growth requires pressure matched with support.

The shell that constrains an embryo protects it too.

Out of Jack's carefully planted bean came a great stalk.

*I'm doing my best to raise my son and give him a
nurturing, loving, and caring environment
so he can grow up and be the best version of himself.*

– Miranda Kerr

Points of Light

Linda – *I found comfort in knowing that there is more to my life than I'm just not good enough. My family had their own struggles and they were not sure what to do about me. I got lost in all their stuff. I didn't know how much impact they had until I read this. They weren't mean, but they were focused on things besides me and my brother and sister. We all sort of fell through the cracks at home. We were all pretty much on our own when it came to school, figuring out social stuff, and trying to make our way through things in our neighborhood. It wasn't a good neighborhood and there were always challenges. I'm not sure my parents understood they needed to be careful with us. I know they didn't. I'm just realizing I have to be careful with myself.*

Janet – *My son was a challenge from day one. He cried as a baby and sleep was always a struggle. I loved him to death, but raising him was like raising two other kids. I was OK with that, but I wish I could have understood a little more of what was going on. School started hard and stayed that way. I had to stay on my son with lots of structure and encouragement. Instinctively, I knew he needed more love and attention than his siblings. They seemed to understand too. They were patient most moments, and only on occasion seemed to resent the extra attention he seemed to always require. Underneath his anger, distraction, and impulsivity was a fragileness I had to remember all the time. I understand better now what he was facing and we were trying to face with him. It's all turned out for him and the family. I think all that love we threw his way compensated for other mistakes and helped him wade through his youth to a pretty good place now.*

Me – _____
_____
_____
_____
_____
_____
_____

CHAPTER THREE

The Gift

Gift [n. gift] A notable capacity, talent, or endowment

The clues that something is up come early – often in disguise. What can seem bad can really be good. We have to look deeper and search for that good. It's always easier to see obstacles than opportunities.

Complexity reveals itself far more often as a difficulty than a lucky break. Amidst the challenges, chaos can easily assert itself as the chief engineer. Things will fail to work when it seems that they should, and when one part appears to be fixed, another can break.

Sometimes we may feel like a fragile, intricate clock competing against the sun's relentless simplicity. In these moments it's easy to get discouraged. Fragility does not lend itself to clarity and confidence.

Human beings are a lot like diamonds, hidden in rocks, buried within mountains. They must be dug up, cut, and polished to reach their full potential.

Complex human beings are diamonds in the rough. . .

He saw mom maybe a dozen times after that day in front of the jail. The visits were mostly nice. She tried to be pleasant and make those random times something special.

Even as a boy he could tell she wanted his approval. She wanted him to be impressed. He was. She was elegant and beautiful – larger than life. But it seemed strange that she wanted his approval almost as much as he wanted hers.

The bad part was that she was constantly telling him how to do things better. He later understood that she was making up for lost time – cramming a year or two of motherhood into a weekend.

Deep down, he also knew she was trying to show him that his dad was doing a bad job and was not teaching him what he needed to learn.

One time, he visited her at her home in Mobile. She and her new attorney husband took him to a nightclub where they had steak and lobster.

There was dancing. At ten years old, he had never danced before. He watched all the adults for a long time before he decided to be brave, to get up and dance – by himself.

He did the twist and thought he was doing it right. After a few songs, he came back to his seat. He expected his mom and the others to be pleased.

Instead, everyone at the table looked at him with disapproval. His mom said, "You don't dance alone – you dance with a partner. Don't you know that?" Her embarrassment was obvious.

He hadn't known that. He hadn't really known how to dance, either. He had tried, and it hadn't gone well. It was many years before he tried again. He was left with a chest brimming full of pain, but he kept on going. . .

No two people are built the same.

Our make-up is as intricate and distinct as a fingerprint.

The deeper one looks, the more truths there are to find.

With complex people, it's necessary to look closer.

We live in a busy and confusing world.

It's easy to look at people and miss the details.

"The desert and the ocean are realms
of desolation on the surface."

– Vera Nazarian

Inconsistency can be a One Percenter flag.

All that internal competition can mess up one's aim.

This inconsistency is often misdefined or badly labeled.

That makes an already difficult situation even worse.

"Overwhelmed" isn't a character trait – it's a consequence.

Complexity does not lend itself to confidence.

It enthusiastically welcomes fear, doubt, and insecurity.

It's tough to feel at ease when life's so hard.

Complexity creates a perfect formula for self-criticism.

One Percenters almost always struggle in this area.

Low self-esteem is a normal part of being exceptional.

Learning to believe in one's own self takes practice.

"There is no substitute for hard work. Never give up.
Never stop believing. Never stop fighting."

– Hope Hicks

Social shyness is not unusual in complex people.

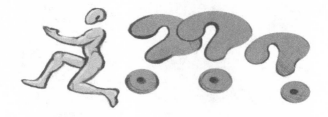

It's hard to embrace others while running from one's self.

Social shyness is a condition – not a character fault.

When we don't understand or even like ourselves,
why should we expect others to react differently?

Facing rejection, it's easy to retreat into a social shell.

Yes, a big vault can hide things of great value.

But our gifts are meant to be visible – not hidden.

"I'm very shy so I became very outgoing to protect my shyness."
– Don Rickles

Sometimes inner turmoil leads us to become actors.

Our days are spent on a stage with a script.

People may like us – but they don't know us.

Although we perform, we never feel safe or close.

That's because people like our mask – not our true selves.

It helps to remember that what we may be hiding are not always flaws, but unique and special potentials.

"The secret of life is honesty and fair dealing. If you can fake that, you've got it made."

– Groucho Marx

Constant inner tension and turmoil is hard.

It can lead to anger.

Anger at our family, anger at our friends, anger at ourselves, anger at the world, anger at God. . .

Anger provides a temporary escape from the pain.

The emphasis is on the word temporary.

Anger is only a distraction from complexity, not an escape.

"Anger is an acid that can do more harm to the vessel in which it is stored than to anything on which it is poured."

– Mark Twain

"Extremes breed extremes" is a reliable truism.

A strong head, heart, hand, and spirit make one busy.

Being too busy inside can produce other extremes.

Some can be strange.

Being strange can lead to being rejected.

Strangeness is often just normalcy when it's overwhelmed.

"Strange how complicated we can make things just to avoid showing what we feel!"

– Erich Maria Remarque

No matter the talents and abilities one has. . .

. . .it is not unusual to never feel good enough.

That's especially true in today's world, where people make it a personal mission to create insecurity in others.

Complex people are more vulnerable to external censure.

It's not possible to criticize others into being better for the same reason stomping on grass doesn't help it grow.

"He has a right to criticize, who has a heart to help."

– Abraham Lincoln

Human beings instinctively like to form groups.

That's okay, but it's not for everyone.

Complex people are less likely to embrace tribes, cliques, teams, groups, or mobs.

They struggle with fear, and they may instinctively resist the entrapping sameness of comfortable conformity.

It's from such people we found that the world is not flat.

"I guess I'm pretty much of a lone wolf. I don't say I don't like people at all but, to tell you the truth I only like it when if I have a chance to look deep into their hearts and their minds."

– Bela Lugosi

Learning new things is difficult for some.

A mind can function either as a sponge or a raincoat.

There is one big reason for this.

Learning first comes as a reminder of what we don't know.

We have to be taught that a lack of knowledge is the first step toward new knowledge. It is not a mark of failure.

Complex brains require encouragement to become spongy, curious, and ready to absorb new stuff.

"Education is the kindling of a flame, not the filling of a vessel."

– Socrates

Points of Light

Jason – *I never did like being in groups. I thought they were like a herd of sheep where a few of the stronger ones ran the show. I didn't like the idea of having to swallow myself to fit in. Down deep inside I knew it was more than that. Part of me wasn't sure I could fit in even if I tried. There were too many things to keep up with; how you dressed, how you talked, and how you acted were yardsticks the "in" people used to measure your worthiness to be part of their group. I think I was right to reject that conformity. I do wish I had tried a little harder to find a few close friends who were also on the outside looking in. But that was when I was in school. I'm out now, and I'm still a non-conformist. I have friends, but I wish I had more and better ones. Finding people with an independent mind who are also friendly and interested in being a friend or having a friend is more difficult than I imagined it would be. I thought that friendships and finding a place to belong came naturally once you were on your own. If anything, it's harder now that I am an adult. I like that thing about the best way to have a friend is to be one. I'm going to work on that.*

Amanda Ann – *Middle school was a crazy time for everybody. I guess being popular helped, but inside I felt like an imposter. I worked hard to hide my insecurities so I could fit it. I saw what happened with the people who didn't. It was like they had a target on their back. They were fair game for any criticism or abuse the rest of us came up with. I tried to be nice to others, but most of my friends didn't. My middle school was the meanest place I have ever been. It was like a movie. Sometimes it seemed like cruelty was more important than learning. That meanness made me afraid to lose my place in the constant popularity contest. I wasn't able to ease up until high school. Things were a little better there, but I've never forgotten middle school. The abuse I saw left me with a permanent fear of other people.*

Me – _____

_____

_____

_____

CHAPTER FOUR

One Percenter Truths

One [adjective. wan] Preeminently what is indicated

Finding one's way through the maze of life is a demanding undertaking for everyone. That tax can be higher for some than it is for others.

Complex people face great expectations, which are rarely matched with great confidence. Ironically, those who have the most to offer frequently believe they have the least.

No one is immune from the hidden pressures of unfulfilled potential. It never goes away and complex people can never escape the pressure of expectation. But hidden bounty is bounty nonetheless.

Our collective mission is to dig it up, much like an exploration team would search for, discover, and recapture buried pirate treasure. It's an all-hands-on-deck kind of adventure. . .

He hated that school. He hated everything about it. Having never known hate, maybe it was just that he hated himself for how miserable he felt every time he walked through those doors.

It was so different than the elementary school he first attended in South Carolina. There he felt safe. Here he felt anything but.

His teacher was young and pretty, but she was also very cold. The students were rough and cruel, and they found apparent satisfaction in relentless criticism.

He was never able to count even one friend at that school.

The Music Man had just come out in theaters and his class was learning the score. They would sing those songs every day. "Seventy-six trombones led the big parade" and other clips from that musical to this day trigger unpleasant memories. Music freezes time.

He learned softball at that school. Not well, but well enough to not always be chosen last. He batted left-handed – and still does because that was the side from which coincidence had him approaching his first uncoached time at bat.

At the end of one particularly hard day of peer abuse, he went to his teacher and asked for advice and help. She responded by simply telling him he was a "chicken" because he didn't fight back. She finished the conversation by closing her grade book, looking at him with disgust. The message was clear: there was nothing else to be said.

He left and never talked to her again – about anything. Even then, he knew that she was wrong. How was someone with no confidence, friends, or knowledge of how to fight supposed to resist someone with super-confidence, lots of friends, and fighting enthusiasm?

He was too embarrassed to let his dad know. He feared that he would give him that same old look of humiliation and that would just amplify the pain. There was nothing to do but swallow the shame and keep on going. . .

Some people are given their place in the world.

Many of us have to find our place in the world.

One Percenters are exceptions to both of these paths.

We have to build our place in the world.

"The best way to not feel hopeless is to get up and do something. Don't wait for good things to happen to you."

– Barack Obama

Complexity creates a vulnerability to misery.

In other words - it's sometimes normal to feel abnormal.

Depression, anxiety and other painful emotions do not affirm inadequacy or punishment for being different.

They are a message telling us we must search for better.

"Hide not your talents, they for use were made.
What's a sundial in the shade?"

– Benjamin Franklin

It's tough to fit in when we feel left out.

There's a natural tendency to isolate.

People aren't designed to be detached from other people.

One Percenters are no exception.

We need "people food" too.

Sometimes, we just have to work harder to find it.

*"You need a team. You need people to push you.
You need opponents."*

– Wynton Marsalis

Complex people naturally have lots of clutter.

There's often a temptation to bury some of it.

But being hidden is not the same thing as being gone.

Buried stuff always surfaces, and not necessarily when, where, or how we want it to.

The stuff we hide has a big impact on who we become.

Sometimes even more impact than what's in plain sight.

"God's voice is still and quiet and easily buried under an avalanche of clamor."

– Charles Stanley

47

We are put on this planet to build things.

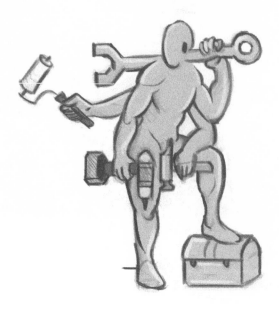

Sometimes those things are physical structures, but they can also be products, opportunities, or ideas.

The most important things require the most talents.

Unleashed, complex people can build remarkable things.

"Every person has a longing to be significant; to make a contribution; to be a part of something noble and purposeful."

– John C. Maxwell

From start to finish, life is about growth.

There is no way around this responsibility.

Complex people have a tougher job with growth.

The more there is to a person, the longer it takes to pull everything together and support our deeper potentials.

Getting to this point can take years – even a lifetime.

But when we do get there, it can be golden.

"If no pain, then no love. If no darkness, no light. If no risk, then no reward."

– Glennon Doyle Melton

Complex people are rarely boring.

There's always something going on.

All those parts have natural cravings that demand attention, opportunity, and nourishment!

One Percenters are sort of like a new litter of kittens.

Released, we are full of life, curiosity, and mischief!

"Now let it work. Mischief, thou art afoot.
Take thou what course thou wilt."

– William Shakespeare

Figuring and setting boundaries is always tough.

Boundaries are the limits we have to place between our world and the world of others.

Setting these limits is the way we learn to live with ourselves, to live with others, and to successfully function in the real world – all at the same time.

It's a difficult juggling act.

"All at the same time" is the toughest part.

"We need to have a talk on the subject of what's yours and what's mine."

– Stieg Larsson, The Girl with the Dragon Tattoo

People with really good brains think a lot.

Sometimes, they think too much. Way too much.

That leads to something called paralysis by analysis.

Bright people often have to retrain their brain.

They have to seek skills that make their brain an asset.

The brain that gets us into trouble can also get us out.

*"The pendulum of the mind oscillates
between sense and nonsense."*

– Carl Jung

Points of Light

Susan – *I really identify with the idea that some of us have to build our place in the world. It doesn't seem fair that other people get things handed to them or are fortunate enough to stumble on a good thing, but I clearly get the fact of life is not always fair. At least my course is clear. I can't wait any longer for my "Fairy Godmother" to wave her wand at me. Now that I know what I am supposed to do, I can get on with it – even though I'm not sure what "it" will be. I want to count for something besides just being here and taking up space. I want to do something useful. I want to have some value. Too many people around me just seem to take up space. Though they seem to be satisfied on the outside, it's hard to understand how. I know that won't work for me. I have this yearning to be something better than I am. I don't feel confident in my search, but I am committed to that need.*

Stephen – *Boring certainly hasn't been part of my life program. I've been in trouble as long as I can remember. Not in big ways, but certainly in "drive my teachers crazy" ways. It's been almost like a life mission to keep things stirred up around me. I'm definitely a non-conformist. Sometimes that's a good thing and sometimes it's not. While others around me wanted to be part of the herd, it suited me to step off to the side and try another way. As I have aged things have become more balanced. I try not to resist just to resist. If I go a different way, and I still do that a lot, I try to do so for good reasons. I'm glad that I tend to walk on my own road. It can be lonely and difficult sometimes, but I feel like that's who I'm supposed to be. Staying positive along the way is important.*

Me – _____

_____

_____

_____

_____

_____

_____

CHAPTER FIVE

Hardspots

Hardspot [n. härd-spät] A state of impairment and uncertainty; confusion; apprehension; distress

We live in a predatory world. No matter how much we wish it were otherwise, there will always be forces seeking to undo us.

Some of our attackers stalk us from the outside. Some ambush us from within. Both hold the power to do great harm.

Complex people have more moving parts and are thus more vulnerable to things that can harm them.

There are some sources of stress that are particularly challenging. . .

At first, that large mill town in Virginia held hope. It was different than the North Carolina village. Things were more positive and open, and the boy wasn't the only new guy.

He remembers the music – Johnny Rivers, Roy Orbison, and Petula Clark. On a portable radio, he tuned into Ft. Wayne's WOWO on the nights there wasn't a hockey game. It made the evenings softer.

So did his James Bond books. He found a bunch in a used book store. As he read them, Bond's life became his path toward a future of hope. A loner like him, Bond did everything right. He knew no fear.

Though things seemed better, the problems at school started in the first week. A guy who had been friendly at first tried to take his lunchroom seat. He refused and was challenged to an after-school fight. The upcoming conflict was a source of dread for the rest of the day.

He tried his hardest, but it wasn't much of a match. The other guy had a bunch of friends and knew how to box. The boy was alone and had no clue on how to defend himself other than to go forward and swing.

He'd been hit about a half-dozen times when a Catholic Priest came out of his rectory and broke things up. He was angry and yelling about fighting on church property.

The priest looked at the young man like he was something evil. In truth, being there was the last thing the boy wanted.

The walk home was lonely, and the boy told no one about what had happened. Why tell people about losing?

That guy and his friends never bothered him again. They more or less ignored him. It was better than being ridiculed. At least he had tried to stand up for himself. But at the end of the day, he was stuck with the fact there was nothing to do but keep going. . .

Complexity lends itself to pain. . .

. . .and people in pain are vulnerable.

It doesn't matter if it's head, heart, hand, or spirit pain.

People in pain struggle.

Pain leaves us with an unavoidably simple choice.

We suffer with it, or we grow from it.

*"But in the end one needs more courage
to live than to kill himself."*

– Albert Camus

People in pain wear masks.

Pain is easier to hide than to handle.

But it is important to remember that pain is like evil.

It festers and grows in the darkness.

People in pain can't be helped without sources of light.

"It is during our darkest moments that
we must focus to see the light."

– Aristotle

People in pain are self-centered.

Focusing on ourselves provides temporary distraction.

But feeling better isn't the same as being better.

Water can never permanently defeat thirst.

Turning inward and trying to change the world is a trap.

Turning outward and changing what's inside works better.

"Every man must decide whether he will walk in the light of creative altruism or in the darkness of destructive selfishness."

– Martin Luther King, Jr.

People in pain withdraw.

There are many reasons to hide.

Fear

Anger

Shame

Confusion

Protection

A garaged car is safe, but that's not what cars are for.

Cars and people are for seeking out opportunities, moving forward, and getting things done.

We can't hide, be safe, and grow all at the same time.

"Security is mostly a superstition. It does not exist in nature. Avoiding danger is no safer in the long run than outright exposure.

– Helen Keller

People in pain sometimes harm themselves.

Ending our life can be a powerful temptation.

Sometimes it's for distraction.

Sometimes it's to beat others to it.

Sometimes it's for self-punishment.

Sometimes it's to just get it over with.

The answer to pain is not more pain.

"The suicide arrives at the conclusion that what he is
seeking does not exist; the seeker concludes that he
has not yet looked in the right place."

– Paul Watzlawick

Sometimes people in pain think they deserve it.

We can also imagine that normal people don't feel the same
pain as strongly or as often as we do.

It's easy to get lost in this skewed perception of pain.

We may see pain as punishment, but pain is rarely about
what we deserve.

More often it is just an unpleasant stimulant for change.

*"Encouragers turn mountains into molehills.
Discouragers turn molehills into mountains."*

– Cathy Burnham Martin

People in pain are almost always addicted

We can become addicted; to almost anything – money, power, drugs, people, worry, food, sex, sleep, screens, celebrities, anger, violence, talking, exercise, laziness, etc.

The list goes on and on.

It's not if we'll become addicted, it's when, to what, and how strongly we will become addicted.

Time strengthens the poison.

Knowledge, discipline, and good choices are the antidote.

"Reality is just a crutch for people who can't handle drugs."

– Robin Williams

People in pain often blame others for their misery.

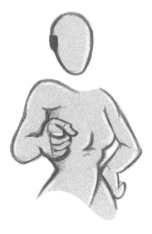

It's easier to blame someone other than ourselves.

But blame isn't productive, no matter who the target is.

It doesn't fix anything.

Repairs take accountability – personal accountability.

We can't fix a flat by just pinpointing the hole.

"Blame is just a lazy person's way of making sense of chaos."
– Douglas Coupland

People in pain often become dependent.

Putting our life into the hands of other things, places, circumstances, or people assures failure.

We and others may pretend it can be done.

But nothing can carry our weight for very long.

Dependency usually makes people angry and demanding.

That's because dependency = powerlessness, and powerlessness = fear, and fear = despair.

"The surest way to be unhappy is to depend on someone else to make you happy."

– Marty Rubin

People in pain usually have sophisticated defenses.

Sophisticated doesn't necessarily mean good.

Building defenses outside stops growth inside.

The door that locks things out also locks things in.

A fort and a prison are much the same.

It depends on who holds the key.

"Watch your back.
Ain't a thing in armor worth trustin' out there."

– Elizabeth Carlton

Learning is a life cornerstone, but there's a catch.

Not everyone learns the same way.

Most learn by seeing, doing, hearing, reading, or writing.
Public education is largely geared to the last three.
That leads to a lot of left-out learners.

How we learn is less crucial than making sure we do learn.

Complex people like to learn in their own way.

The key is learning to blend our way with society's way.

*"Continuous effort - not strength or intelligence -
is the key to unlocking our potential."*

– Winston Churchill

Points of Light

Joe – *I really liked the part about wearing a mask to hide myself. I do that and thought I was the only one who did. Well, not really the only one, but certainly one of very few that I know. I definitely do it to hide my pain. Sometimes I hurt so much I think I'm going to explode. I don't, but it feels like I could. I'm afraid that if I reveal that part of me to others that they will think I am weak or weird. I also understand that I have to take that mask down sometimes and let people see the real me. I immediately assume people will not like me just like they didn't like me when I was a kid and really don't like me even now. Taking off my mask is a hard thing to do, but I get it. I was thinking about who I might do that with, who I could trust. It's going to be hard, but I get the need. I'm going to have to take somebody's word for it that I can't do this alone.*

Cyndi – *Reading this section had me feeling like I could check off "all of the above" when it came to "hardspots." It was a little discouraging until I realized the real emphasis was not on the hardspots, but the antidotes to the hardspots. I got nailed on the page about blaming others for my misery. I do that on the outside, but on the inside I mostly blame myself. It was helpful to read it doesn't really matter who I blame, because blaming others or myself doesn't get me anywhere. I'm trying to pick up on the suggestion that my power lies in being responsible and searching for solutions. I especially liked that part about fixing a flat by only searching for the hole. I do that. I'm working hard to stop.*

Me – _____

_____

_____

_____

_____

_____

_____

_____

_____

_____

_____

CHAPTER SIX

A Helping Hand

* Help [v. hlp] To give assistance to someone; make it easier to do something; aid...

Complex people have the same vulnerabilities as everyone else, but they are different in that those vulnerabilities are often magnified.

That's why engaged supporters like parents, teachers, counselors, coaches, ministers, siblings, and friends play such a crucial and often unappreciated role in the life of One Percenters. They create bridges through difficult waters.

One truism applies to all complex people: we never reach our potential alone. . .

He was back in his hometown of Asheville in the eighth grade.

Something changed while he was there. Things weren't any better inside, and his family was still in turmoil, but he found some friends in his neighborhood and at school. That made all the difference.

There were guys to learn from and hang out with. Curiously, even their families made him feel welcomed in their homes. It was a strange change, but it felt good.

Yes, there were the usual bullies and critics, but not nearly as many. His school was actually a pretty happy place. They had sock-hops, pep rallies, and other fun activities. The teachers liked what they were doing and tried to be helpful. He made good grades.

But there were still bad memories. One came – per usual – from his father. The boy and a friend hid a cigar in the attic. They would take a couple of puffs and then put it out, saving the rest for another day. It was their own secret way of visiting the adult world that flourished around them.

On Christmas Eve he went to his grandparents to open gifts. He was one of the first to be handed a present. He noticed everyone seemed extra intent when he began to unwrap his "gift."

Inside the package, he found his cigar and the cup he kept it in.

He felt like he had been kicked when he looked at it. He lifted his head to his father's smirking face – it was a look of satisfaction that said, "I sure taught you a lesson."

But all his father really did was build up another layer of shame and sorrow.

In many ways, that was the last day he really had a dad. The cruelty in those eyes severed a connection that was irreplaceable. He was more alone than ever, but he kept on going. . .

Every human has an emotional processor, not unlike a data processor in a home computer.

That processor is built in the first three years of life.

Dads, step-moms, adopted parents, foster parents, and others can help, but the single most important role in building a child's capacity to effectively process emotions belongs to the biological mom.

If she's not available, or doesn't do a good or complete job, we have to finish developing our own emotional processor.

Filling in the gaps is often a life-long undertaking.

And it's much easier to learn at three than it is at thirty.

In the end, we have to take over where mom leaves off.

"Failure is a bend in the road, not the end of the road. Learn from failure and keep moving forward."

– Roy T. Bennett

We are brought into this world by design.

We have a place and a mission.

Complex people often resent this assignment.

It's hard to face so much pressure from within and without.

But big world problems need even bigger people.

"Your dream is to feel good; God's dream is for you to do good."

– Shannon L. Alder

All cultures are not healthy.

Loyalty to a corrupt social culture can, in turn, corrupt us.

Cultures, like people, can grow toward darkness or light.

It's a mistake to believe all are good.

Good potentials do not always assure a good outcome.

Cultural dedications must be made with wisdom and care.

Like plants, we should grow toward cultures of light.

"We can easily forgive a child who is afraid of the dark; the real tragedy of life is when men are afraid of the light."

– Plato

Families are the linchpin of any healthy culture.

But not all families are healthy.

A family is an incubator.

Dysfunctional families can be harmful incubators.

Without repair, damage and its impact can last a lifetime.

Coming from a broken family hands us a harsh reality.

We are in charge of the repair work.

"One needn't stop dysfunction; just evince and reflect."

– Andy Harglesis

The gift of life comes with a hidden pressure.

We are under constant pressure to keep reaching.

Life is built around a hidden formula.
The gap between our potential and our reality = discomfort.
The bigger the gap, the greater the unhappiness.

We thus face a relentless calling.
Not to be better than others, but to be an ever better us.

Happiness comes at a cost. We must bring our gifts to life.

"I was doing something I'd never done before. And what will I be able to do tomorrow that I cannot yet do today?"

– Elizabeth Gilbert

We live in a marvelously self-correcting world.

It constantly filters out the bad and rewards the good.

We have to be sure we make the cut.
Bad choices put us at risk for a bad outcome.

Being good is not an accident – it is an active decision.

No one can save us from the need to make that decision.

Those who try are enablers, and they only make us smaller.

"Do your little bit of good where you are; it's those little bits of
good put together that overwhelm the world."

– Desmond Tutu

75

Caring people are skilled in easing other's pain.

Yet we must be careful.

Help can easily turn into indulgence.

Coddling the inadequacies of others makes them weaker.

There's a big difference between patience and pampering.

It's tricky, but helpers must serve love with accountability.

To do otherwise is to condemn with invisible abuse.

"What children need is the conviction that satisfaction can and must be earned. Spoiled children do not learn the must."

– Isabel Briggs Myers

People are like fruit.

We are alike, but different.

Some are sweet – some are sour.

Some are soft – some are firm.

Some are good – some are bad.

Bad fruit can turn good fruit into bad fruit.

One bad apple spoils the barrel.

Who we rub against matters.

We have to be careful about how we take time out.

Nature insists we remain fully engaged in the real world.

Intoxicants, artificial environments, fantasy, materialism, addictions, and other distractions can help us feel better, but they only offer temporary relief.

There is no true, lasting escape from life's obligations.

Finding balance is about persistence, not perfection.

It's where we live, not visit, that determines our future.

"By prevailing over all obstacles and distractions, one may unfailingly arrive at his chosen goal or destination."

– Christopher Columbus

Pleasure is a false god that leads many astray.

We are culturally encouraged to worship pleasure.

Feeling good is first and foremost a by-product.
It comes from being good and doing good.

Putting pleasure first in our lives leads to despair.

The reason is simple.

Pleasure and growth rarely travel on the same train.

"We have had enough, once and for all, of Hedonism – the
gloomy philosophy which says that pleasure is the only good."

– C. S. Lewis

Life is not a perfect or predictable process.

It ebbs and flows like the ocean tides.

We float at times, and we paddle at others.

Awkward moments are guaranteed

This is particularly true for complex people.

That's what happens when four oceans come together.

"In chaos, there is fertility."

– Anais Nin

Pain is a reality of living in a hard world.

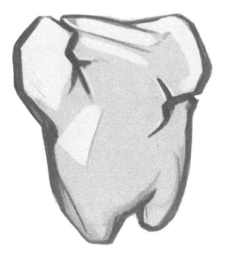

Pain may come to our head, heart, hand, or spirit.

Much like a toothache, pain comes to warn us.

It helps to remember pain is a foundation for growth.
It helps to remember that most pain is temporary.
It helps to remember that we're not powerless in our pain.

There's a reason.

God always hides opportunity amidst misery.

"Out of suffering have emerged the strongest souls; the most
massive characters are seared with scars."

– Kahlil Gibran

Points of Light

Andrea – *I'm a guidance counselor. I've always thought that some of the students I see didn't get a fair reading on their potentials. Though they struggled with some things, there were strengths underneath. It's nice to have a way to frame up these special students. They get a raw deal most of the time. Our academic system is set up for the average or above-average who fit in. A lot of students, maybe most students, don't fit into that box. It's not that the box is bad. We do a lot of good things for our kids. It's just hard to cover the needs of everyone. This gives me a framework to use in explaining some students to teachers who struggle to find answers on how best to help. I like it that a lost group has their path defined in a positive way. It's not about a new label. It's about a way to understand and help others to reach for a better outcome. I'm grateful for a new tool in my very full toolbox.*

Jerry – *I was definitely an angry young man. I look back at my school pictures and all I see is a sullen guy looking like he hated everything about his life. That's pretty much what I did feel – a whole lot of hate. I hated school, I hated my family, I hated my town, I hated life, and I hated me. I can see now that depression and fear were at the root of my anger. It felt better than feeling weak and inadequate all the time. It was the only tool I had for fighting back. It wasn't until in my twenties that I began to find a better way. The less competitive nature of young adulthood and a few new friends helped. I got a job right after high school and found out I could work harder than most people. I was rewarded for my effort and that led to other opportunities and growth opportunities. I still had a temper that would come out of me unannounced, but I didn't like it in the same way I once did. It took me a while, but I've come to understand that there was more to me than just being a p**sed-off guy. This book is opening my eyes on where that anger came from, and what I can keep trying to do to move beyond it.*

Me – _____

_____

_____

_____

_____

_____

_____

CHAPTER SEVEN

More Care and Feeding

* Care [v. kär] Feel concern or interest; attach importance to
something...

There are certain things that can be done to aid complex
people on their exceptional journey. Think of these as essential
vitamins and minerals for the head, heart, hand, and spirit. We
don't need them all at the same time and in the same doses, but
we definitely can't make it without them . . .

James Bond never had it easy, but he always seemed to have it good.

The boy was thirteen when he first saw Goldfinger. He'd been reading Ian Fleming's books since he was eleven and thought he knew what was coming. Nothing could have prepared him for that night at the drive-in.

The movie was simply magnificent! Every moment was extraordinary and larger than life – better than he had ever imagined life could be.

Bond had power, opportunity, adventure, love, and value at a level that was inconceivable. His control, clarity, courage, and conviction were revelations to a struggling pre-teen.

There was more out there than life as it was for him.

It was Mr. Fleming and Mr. Bond who gave him a role model – and just as importantly, a distraction from the dullness of the ordinary and the pain of being trapped in the misery.

The boy met other larger than life characters. The Man from U.N.C.L.E., The Avengers, and Secret Agent were heaven-sent guides to help him escape. They weren't Bond, but they were there every week.

On Friday nights, a loaf of French bread and quart of ginger ale became his makeshift European cuisine and Champagne. He would eat while he watched them back-to-back on his black and white television. It became a dependable sanctuary – he could lose himself in that temporary glamour and intrigue.

It wasn't that he thought he could be like Bond or the others. It was just comforting to know that there were people out there like that. Maybe he, too, could become a little bit like them. At a time when the pain was at its worst, knowing that he might grow to be more helped him to keep on going. . .

Validation

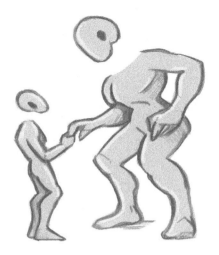

Recognition helps build identity and keeps us moving forward. It provides understanding on what works. It knits our abilities and skills together. It eases the pain of errors.

Validation is food.

Without it, we starve.

The lasting impact of validation is easily affirmed.

We learn to value ourselves first by being valued by others.

"To need to be seen, to be heard, to be understood,
is simply to be human."

– L.R. Knost

Successes

Complex people have a lot to master.

A sense of our ability to achieve in the outside world is necessary for our sense of value on the inside.

Success sparks growth, motivation, hope, and reach.

Success is not everything, and it cannot fix everything.

But it is a very necessary thing for growth and hope.

"As long as you keep going, you'll keep getting better. And as you get better, you gain more confidence. That alone is success."

– Tamara Taylor

Safety

Complex people sometimes make for easy targets.

Complex people already feel unsafe inside.

That makes outside safety doubly important.

Protection by others, as well as skills in emotional and physical self-protection, are equally essential.

Nothing is possible without a safe foundation. Nothing.

"In ourselves our safety must be sought.
By our own right hand it must be wrought."

— William Wordsworth

Structure

Chaos can be the enemy of complexity.

Jell-O without a mold will never set up.

Too much structure chokes.
Too little structure scatters.
The right measure supports growth the right way.

The search for 'just right' never ends.

*"In your hands I am no longer a pile of bones
left behind to a world that moved on."*

– Taylor Patton

Clarity

We can't work on what we don't understand.

Knowing who we are and where we are is a foundation for
getting where we're meant to go.

Complexity settles around us like a hazy fog.

Clarity blows that fog away.

"When the meaning is unclear there is no meaning."

– Marty Rubin

Growth

This is a crucial word for complex people.

There is no escape from our need to grow.

There is a reason we are forced to improve.

It is only through growth that we build our potentials.

After all, we are here to touch the world.

Everyone has to grow into that role.

"Everyone wants to live on top of the mountain, but all the happiness and growth occurs while you're climbing it."

– Andy Rooney

Opportunity

Beckoning doors are an essential piece to life's puzzle.

No new doors means no new growth.

Opportunity + Action = Potential for new growth.

We all need door builders, guides, and motivators.

We must also press our courage button and walk through.

"If opportunity doesn't knock, build a door"

– Milton Berle

Love

In a hard world, there's a big need for soft spots.

Love is the softest spot of all.
Not just love we get – but also the love we give.

It's true:

The greatest thing we ever learn –

is just to love – and be loved in return.

"Being deeply loved by someone gives you strength, while loving someone deeply gives you courage."

– Lao Tzu

Grace

Every human being is graced with an inner spirit.

That spirit is liberated by light, strangled by darkness.

A liberated inner spirit brings joy, purpose, and protection.

A strangled spirit leads to despair, emptiness, and anger.

The grace of an inner spirit is free, but its potentials are unleashed through faith and good choices.

The neglected spirit is a garden for weeds.

"The Spirit of God breathes inspiration,
while the carnal mind breeds vanity."

– Fred C. White

Points of Light

Mary Louise – *The idea that I needed to actively work on growing is something new to me. I know it seems obvious, but I thought growth was natural, not something you had to work at. It's sort of dawning on me that I, maybe more than some, have to be very purposeful about growing. I need to make up for lost time spent doubting myself and then there are all those gaps in who I am. I get the idea that I may have more parts than some people and that pulling all that together is not something one should leave to chance. So, starting right now, growing myself is going way up front on my list of priorities. It feels hopeful to think that way.*

Tonya – *I've thought about dying a lot. In fact, I sometimes think about dying more than I think about anything else. It seems like a way out. If I wasn't afraid, I would actually be dead by now. I find life so hard that sometimes it's just hard to understand how to keep doing it. I understood the different reasons people in pain sometimes harm themselves. For me it's the last one – I'd like to get life over with. But then comes that last sentence, "The answer to pain is not more pain." Could dying not really be the end of the pain? I'm afraid to take the chance and that keeps me going. I also don't want to hurt my family and others. I've always noticed that when people die by suicide there seems to be an extra dose of sadness and pain for those who are left behind. I get it that the answer is trying to grow through the pain – and that I have to keep trying. I will, but I wish it was easier.*

Me – _____

_____

_____

_____

_____

_____

_____

_____

_____

_____

CHAPTER EIGHT

Hurdles

* Hurdle [n. hər-d l] An artificial barrier over which racers
must leap...

No life is ever like a fairy tale. It's rarely as simple as facing challenges and then going off to live happily ever after.

From start to finish, every existence is reliably filled with tests. They may change, but they never stop.

Complex people are met with a simple truth about life's hurdles: the complexity of our make-up is reflected in the complexity of our challenges . . .

It was a new school again. A new school, but with the same people he had struggled with several years back. He had changed – they hadn't. It was still the same old mockery, rejection, and threats.

That first year was raw misery. He laid out of school and skipped his classes whenever he could. That was often, because he had obtained a fake report card to cover the ruse.

Everything fell apart at the end of the year. He turned in the real one and the fake one on separate days. He was met with more shame from his parents, but the principal was surprisingly compassionate. Over time, that strong, thoughtful man's quiet support became a lifeline.

Then there was the fighting. The first time he stood up to a long line of challenges is still fresh in his memory. He followed his antagonist into a bathroom and was immediately hit so hard he thought his head would explode. It didn't, but it did motivate him to start hitting back, repeatedly, until someone broke it up.

He left that bathroom feeling elated and different. He hadn't started the fight, but he had held his own better than he would have imagined he could. He wasn't proud of the fight; he was proud that he hadn't backed down from this latest adversary.

It was the beginning of a long line of fistfights with a long line of opponents. It's that way when you're insecure, weigh 140 pounds, and are surrounded by people who are accustomed to raising their esteem by lowering yours.

The fighting at school led to an unpredicted outcome at home: a threat by his father to send him to a psychiatrist. It didn't matter that, with rare exceptions, he was always on the receiving end of bullying. He couldn't win at home, but he did begin to win some of those fights. So, he resolved he would certainly keep on going. . .

Life is hard.

For everyone – in every way.

Complexity can make it even harder.

No one gets a pass.

But we all get opportunity.

The charge is to press forward and cash it in.

"Never confuse a single defeat with a final defeat."

– F. Scott Fitzgerald

There are mean people in the world.

Not most people, but a lot of people.

They are usually miserable people who seek out the vulnerable and impaired as outlets for their virus.

Complex people are vulnerable works in progress and thus are often singled out as targets for social predators.

And so we are stuck with a harsh reality.

We have to learn, with help, to face our antagonists.

"Rudeness is the weak man's imitation of strength."

– Eric Hoffer

The world is complex too.

Our Complexity + World Complexity = Great Difficulty

It's a bit like trying to comb your hair on a roller coaster.

There is no true sanctuary from this reality.

We all have to put our own puzzle together.

Then we have to match it to the bigger world puzzle.

All the while, both puzzles are evolving.

It takes time to figure out how the pieces snap together.

"Life isn't about finding yourself. Life is about creating yourself."
– George Bernard Shaw

Reason does not guide most human behavior.

And mankind's folly is often startling and disappointing.

We will be let down frequently in life, and it will seem that confusion and darkness must surely prevail.

We are here to counter that confusion and darkness, not to surrender to it or become part of it.

That mission is aided by remembering evil strangles itself.

"May the forces of evil become confused on the way to your house."

– George Carlin

Fairy dust salesmen come in many forms.

All are deceivers marketing fantasy over reality.

Fairy dust does not exist.

There is <u>nothing</u> that relieves us of the need to face reality.

Trying to dodge it is like running from a shadow.

The idea of the tooth fairy is appealing, but the dollar under the pillow always comes from a loving hand in the real world, not a fairy from another.

Behind every one of Disney's delights are real people.

"We live in a fantasy world, a world of illusion.
The great task in life is to find reality."

– Iris Murdoch

Trust is an overrated human commodity.

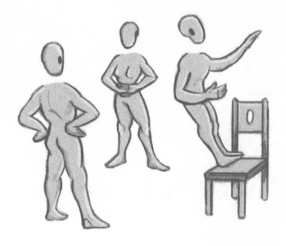

That's because many people are not very trustworthy.

They will let us down when we're counting on them most.

Still, as people ourselves, we need other people.

Taking the risk to trust requires we learn to trust ourselves.

That's the only earthbound trust that is truly trustable.

"When you stop expecting people to be perfect,
you can like them for who they are."

– Donald Miller

If you had four ears, would you listen with them?

We all have a head, heart, hand, and spirit, yet most of us
only listen with small, dominant parts of our head.

That may seem to make sense, but it means we miss a lot.

The heart, hand, and spirit know things too.
Sometimes they know things the brain can't begin to know.

Life etches the head, heart, hand, and spirit with
remarkably crafted and accessible wisdom.

But to benefit, we must listen to them all carefully.

"There is a wisdom of the head & a wisdom of the heart."

– Charles Dickens

Failure is inevitable.

There are three truths about failure:

It is not a permanent condition.

It produces as much growth as harm.

Failing doesn't make you a failure.

The only truly harmful failures are failing to try, failing to learn, and failing to press on.

Facing and riding out our failures can be our best success.

*"All of old. Nothing else ever. Ever tried. Ever failed.
No matter. Try again. Fail again. Fail better."*

– Samuel Becket

Motivation is not an abundant human resource.

There's a reason.

We get the motivation equation twisted around backwards.

We typically think motivation produces action, but it's actually the reverse that's true.

Action produces motivation.

The more you do, the more you will be motivated to do!

Motivated people thus have a key: They keep on doing!

"Do it badly; do it slowly; do it fearfully;
do it any way you have to, but do it."

– Steve Chandler

It's a scary world.

And it seems to be getting scarier.

Our fear button is pushed relentlessly.

That's okay, because there's an antidote.

Practice pressing your courage button more than the world presses your fear button.

"Scared is what you're feeling. Brave is what you're doing."

– Emma Donoghue

Addictions are a relentless lurking concern.

They hide and wait everywhere, like monsters in a child's closet – except that in this case, they are real.

An addiction is anything that crowds out normal living by helping us evade pain and responsibility.

Escaping our burdens is an understandable temptation.

But when we take our first step toward giving in, hope for our future begins an immediate retreat.

"There are all kinds of addicts, I guess. We all have pain. And we all look for ways to make the pain go away."

– Sherman Alexie

The will to live can be slippery.

The harms, hardness, and hurdles of life can pile up.

Sometimes those hazards seem overwhelming.

The imagined peace of death can be appealing.

It's not necessarily that we want to die so much as we are willing to take excessive steps to escape the pain.

There's an alternative.

We must find ways to defeat our pain instead of our life.

"If your heart is still beating, God is not done with you yet."

- Dillon Burroughs

Points of Light

John – *I'm addicted to so many things, I don't know where to start. There's weed, anger, withdrawal, junk food, and so many others I can't even count them. When I think about it I realize I've been relying on my addictions to get me by since I was a teenager. Video games and TV carried me until I discovered alcohol. It made me feel normal. It still does, except I'd like to feel normal some other way. Marijuana took over when I was about seventeen. I've been smoking it daily or even more than once a day since then. I don't get the same relief I once did. In fact I hate weed now. I never thought I would ever say that. It was so good to me for years. Now, I hate the smell, the money it costs, the lifestyle, and even the numbness it produces. My problem is I don't know what I can use to replace it. I've relied on it for so long to cope that even a day without smoking a bowl is hard and strange. I may start on some of my easier addictions first.*

Alice – *I liked hearing that failure and fear are normal. I've always felt like I was uniquely overloaded with a tendency to fail and more fears than I can count. The idea that failure can be a foundation for growth makes sense, but for me, it just seems like a foundation for more failure and shame. Fear follows me wherever I go. I'm afraid when I'm alone, when I'm with people I know, and when I'm with people I don't know. It's funny though, I'm not as afraid of strangers as I am people I am close to. I guess it's because strangers haven't hurt me as much as my own family and friends have hurt me. Getting close sometimes feels like a decision to step into a shooting gallery. Strangers can be a temporary source of human interaction without all the risks that go with getting close to people. I understand that people need people though. I certainly do.*

Me – _____
_____
_____
_____
_____
_____
_____

CHAPTER NINE

The Package...

* Package [n. pakij] Something conceived of as a compact unit having particular characteristics.

You've heard it many times before – human beings are amazing creatures. Our remarkable combination of parts makes us extraordinarily capable.

Unfortunately, those capabilities can be devoted to harm as surely as good. To do the most good, we have to make use of all the parts we have and invest them wisely.

We come into the world as a package deal. Our head, heart, hand, and spirit are intertwined and inter-reliant in so many ways that it's impossible to always get it right.

Fortunately, when it comes to managing ourselves, perfection isn't necessary – only excellence. Why excellence? Because it seems the next level of achievement is mediocrity, and it's just a short hop from 'mediocre' to 'dysfunctional.'

This is especially true for One Percenters – if you're not working to reach for really good, you're probably drifting toward something bad.

Keeping all that complexity on the straight and narrow is a demanding balancing act. Here are some head-heart-hand-spirit clues on how to do it. . .

The Head...

He remembered the first time he realized he might not be as dumb as he believed, or as others suggested.

It was in high school. One of his English and Literature teachers had a reputation for being stern and no-nonsense, but for some reason, she was always nice to him. She was encouraging and frequently made positive notes on his papers.

He learned why years later. It seemed that during the summers this teacher would go through the aptitude test scores looking for students performing below their measured ability.

She pegged him as one of those underperformers and took him on as an unwitting project. Her mission was quietly relayed to his sister by the principal – an added unrewarded kindness.

He wished he had known earlier so he could have properly thanked Ms. Perly. Probably more than anyone, she pushed him toward his learning potentials. He didn't do well in class, but at least he began to understand he had the ability to do better. If he could go back in time, he would say something like this —

"Thank you, Ms. Perly. You may like knowing that when I joined the service after graduation, I tested out of college level English and Literature. That traces firmly to your hand."

Thanks to a silent and timely boost from a very tough, very special lady, he was able to keep on going. . .

Many people have a spoiled brain.

It thinks when it wants to, with or without permission.

The bigger the mind, the more it wants to think.

The brain is naturally suited to the role of pestering bully.

It likes to push our other parts aside.

So, it's important that the brain knows something.

We run it; it doesn't get to run us.

"Worry does not empty tomorrow of its sorrow.
It empties today of its strength."

– Corrie Ten Boom

Thinking comes naturally.

Productive thinking doesn't.

We have to train our brain to think in this way.

Creativity, problem solving, meditation, and learning are all examples of productive thinking.

Worry, obsession, and agitation aren't.

"Inspiration exists, but it has to find you working."

— Picasso

Sometimes we must think without thinking.

It's similar to watching a train pass without getting on.

Sometimes we can stop thoughts, but much of the time it's best to just let them go on their way.

They're our thoughts; we can engage with them or not.

Picture having the TV on, but not watching it.

"You can't stop the waves, but you can learn to surf."

– Jon Kabat-Zin

Our brain is designed like a car motor.

It's not supposed to run all the time.

Sometimes it's off.
Sometimes it's idling.
Sometimes it's going slow.
Sometimes it's going fast.

When it comes to our brains, we have to control the motor.

Learning to drive a brain takes lots of practice.

"Stop thinking, and end your problems."

— Lao Tzu

Overstimulation can artificially quicken the brain.

It's easy for our mind to get stuck in the ON position.

Televisions, video games, phones, computers, and other technologies are brain stimulants.

Too much stimulation over a long or frequent time leads to addiction – both to thinking and technology.

In the 21 st century, balancing technology is a crucial skill.

"The difference between technology and slavery is that slaves are fully aware that they are not free"

– Nassim Nicholas Taleb

The Heart...

It never made any sense to him. Why did so many things seem scary, hurtful, or sad? Why did he seem to feel those negative feelings so much more strongly than those around him?

People were always telling him he was too sensitive, that he needed to develop a thicker skin. What did that mean? How was he supposed to do it?

What he did have some success with – at times – was trying to feel nothing at all. Numb emptiness bordering on depression was better than agony.

It never lasted. There was always something to trigger emotion, and when he felt something, it was usually bad.

At some point, he figured out that his tendency to hate himself was connected to the pain. Other people may have triggered emotions, but the pain always landed on him.

Who is more responsible – the person who causes the pain, or the one who feels it?

Early on, he decided it was his inadequacy that made him such an easy target for pain. There was something broken in him, and it couldn't be seen or explained or found in others.

Thoughts of harming himself were frequent. For some reason he couldn't find the right amount of will at the right time. In spite of the endless parade of pain and his inability to stop it, there was only one thing he could really do. He kept on going. . .

Emotions are not right or wrong, good or bad.

What we do with emotions determines that measure.

It's necessary to let ourselves feel what we feel to avoid building up emotional baggage.

But the way we translate those feelings into behavior is where self-control is important, even crucial.

Light and dark are created by the friction of action.

"But feelings can't be ignored, no matter how unjust or ungrateful they seem."

– Anne Frank

Emotions can be stimulated by many things.

One thing is always true – we're the one who feels them.

When we're in pain, it's easy to turn on ourselves.

Toxic exposure to too much pain is a self-esteem killer.

It's crucial that we learn to stop measuring our worth by how we feel, in order to more fairly value who we are.

It's what we do, not feel, that truly measures our worth.

"Feelings are something you have; not something you are."

– Shannon L. Alder

We all have an internal emotional processor.

Many of us aren't blessed with a fully functional one.

That leaves us with three options:

- Enduring the resulting emotional pain and moodiness
- Relying on addiction to escape those feelings
- Working to repair our processor

That's it. There's really nothing else that works.

Guess who has to be the chief mechanic?

"The sun always shines above the clouds."

– Paul F. Davis

One addiction stands out above all others.

That would be the simple desire to feel good.

At its best, feeling good is a byproduct of doing good.

When we skip doing good and pursue feeling good as our primary mission, we inevitably start doing badly.

That's not to say that we can't enjoy life.

It's just that we have to earn our happiness, not steal it.

"Happiness is not something ready-made.
It comes from your own actions."

– Dalai Lama

There are five ways to process painful emotions.

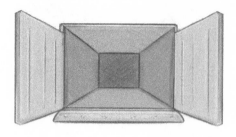

We can run from them.

We can replace them.

We can act them out.

We can bury them.

We can feel them.

Whenever we run (distract ourselves), replace (think swapping anger for hurt), act out (indulge), or bury (suppress), we are left with a troubling fact.

None of these approaches to emotions works very well.

The only way to get free of emotion is to experience it.

Every other approach puts our emotions into storage.

Once there, they lay inside us as an unpleasant lump.

And one day they will surely bubble to the surface.

"The long-term pain suffered by suppressing emotions is far greater than the short-term pain of confronting them."

– Sam Owen

The Hand...

His father could do anything. Every problem he put his hand to was solved. He built, he created, and made everything better. He wasn't so good with people, but he was great with things.

He wasn't a teacher – he was a doer. When you helped him, your job was to bring him tools, hold his light, or anticipate his next need. Learning from him was an incidental thing...except for when he occasionally wanted to pass on knowledge.

He knew a lot, and he would ask his son questions: did he notice him pumping the car's brakes as a way to signal the person behind him? Did he pick up on walking heel to toe so as to not scare the wildlife? Did he understand that you had to keep your speed up while driving in snow to keep from getting stuck?

No matter what the son did, the father could always do it better. In fact, his father made it a point to prove it – every time and in every way. It took years for the boy to realize that his father was competing with him. It was a strange notion...a person who could do everything felt he had to outdo a person who couldn't do anything.

The boy tried to learn the good from his father, and there was much good to learn. It wasn't easy to walk in that shadow, but he had no real choice. He kept on going. . .

Everyone who lives stumbles.

Shame and embarrassment are usually a consequence.

Ridicule from others can magnify that pain.

It's important to pick back up and resist shame's echo.

We are here to live and learn...not to be mistake-proof.

Everyone plays the fool sometimes.

"A life spent making mistakes is not only more honorable, but more useful than a life spent doing nothing."

– George Bernard Shaw

Laying our hand on the world is a risky business.

We can mess up and there are often consequences.

Attempting to avoid rejection can result in perfectionism.

Perfectionists aim real high, but they never make it.
Achievers aim just as high, and they don't make it either.

The important difference: perfectionists focus on what
they didn't accomplish – achievers focus on what they did.

Aim high, but aim as an achiever, never as a perfectionist.

"Perfectionism is self-abuse of the highest order."

– Anne Wilson Schaef

Nastiness is a growing cultural phenomenon.

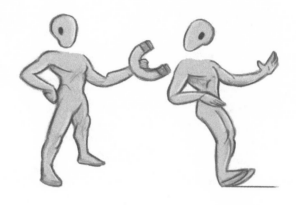

But we can't do good things through bad means.

Nastiness is a short-lived source of power, confidence, impact, and attention. In the long-term, it dries us up.

Patience, creativity, love, productivity, gratitude, and maturity are all special counters to nastiness.

Importantly, nasty people crash into their own extremes.

The counter to nastiness is the quiet power of niceness.

"The right thing to do and the hard thing to do are usually the same."

– Steve Maraboli

Activity is an irreplaceable stimulant for good.

Activity kindles our brain, comforts our heart, trains our hand, and liberates our spirit.

It is the best medicine for most things, most of the time.

In contrast, an overdose of inactivity is poison.

This is extra true for complex people.

Activity helps us grow and knit our pieces together.

"Intelligence must be in the hands
and feet as well as in the head."

– Marty Rubin

Mistakes are inevitable.

Complexity only makes mistakes more inevitable.

Learning from and forgiving errors is important for the same reason it's crucial to clear ice from a plane's wings.

We can't climb to our potentials with too much guilt and misery weighing down our wings.

Everyone stumbles, and we must pick up and press on

Where we're going is more vital than where we've been!

"We learn from failure, not from success!"

– Bram Stoker, Dracula

Every stage of life requires a different level of skill.

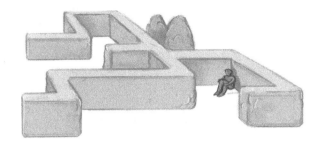

Potty problems are OK at age two – not so much at age ten.

Hurdles need to be reasonably matched to abilities.

This is especially true for complex people.

It's hard to juggle both inside and outside challenges.

It helps to remember to set a proper compass setting.

Between too little and too much is a place that's just right.

"When people complain of your complexity, they fail to remember that they made fun of your simplicity."

– Michael Bassey Johnson

The Spirit...

Graduation from high school meant one thing above all others: liberation. He was free from the captivity and uncertainty.

It didn't last long. He joined the Air Force within weeks of finishing high school. This time he was a volunteer.

Basic Training wasn't hard. In school, he had attempted football and track and was in shape. Surprisingly, he was the second-fastest of fifty guys. It was an unexpected payoff from athletic efforts mostly marked by inadequacy.

After Basic, there was intelligence school followed by a unique assignment on a large Army post. There, a group of Rangers taught him how to parachute – an intimidating hurdle matched to his decision to volunteer for Vietnam.

When he first arrived at that country's point of entry – Camp Alpha – there were 125,000 American troops in country. When he left a year later there were somewhere around 15,000. In the middle was chaos. That's how surrender works, even when the pretense is peace.

His time in Vietnam was marked by captivity and uncertainty of a different nature than he had experienced in school. He was eighteen and excited in the beginning...at the end, much older, and much more confused.

The imprints were too deep for an easy transition. He brought home a sense of pessimism and mistrust. There was so much waste, deception, and damage. His skepticism for the things of man – including government – deepened.

On reflection, he gained more than he lost. As is always the case with service in foreign wars, there was much to learn. One bit of repeated wisdom stood out. In the face of hurdles and hardship, we all have to keep on going. . .

Spiritual people are revealed

most surely by one thing.

They seek the truth.

Spirituality is the search for the deeper meaning of life.

Where do we come from?

What should we be doing while we are here?

Where are we going when we leave here?

Like most hard things, spirituality requires a leap of faith.

That leap is fraught with obstacles.

Like untying the things of man from the things of God.

"But the fruit of the Spirit is love, joy,
peace, patience, kindness, goodness, faithfulness..."

- Galatians 5:22

We all have this little extra something inside us.

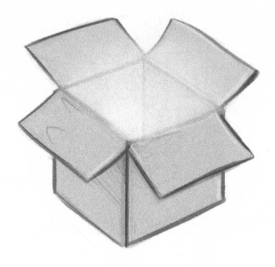

Some call it a conscience; others the holy spirit.

It's our bridge to God – a gift that has to be unwrapped.

Think of a porch. There's a package waiting for us there.

We have to open the door to pick it up.

"Spiritual surrender means you don't try to negotiate the terms."

– S. Lawson

We live in the middle of a spiritual battleground.

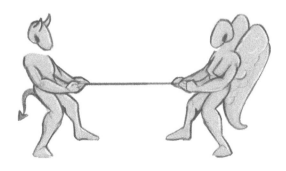

The fight is between good and evil, darkness and light.

No one is granted immunity from the struggle.

We will serve one side or the other.

It's a matter of choice first, and then of practice.

"There is a good dog and a bad dog fighting within each of us.
The one that is going to win is the one we feed the most"

– Chinese Proverb

People are like tables.

Uneven legs make us wobbly.

The head, heart, hand, and spirit all help hold us up.

The one we can't see, the spirit, is easiest to neglect.

That one leg can make all the rest insecure.

Sure, we can make a three-legged table work, but why?

A stable table rests best on four legs.

"Look at the napkins under the table legs."

– Trip Advisor

Life is hard and it's easy to resent the one we have.

But all is not as it seems.

What seems like a good hand can be a bad one.
What seems like a bad hand can be a good one.
And any hand can be played poorly or well.

We first have to put our cards in order...all of our cards.

Then we can play them to the best of our ability.

A sound inner spirit is crucial to doing that wisely.

"Life is like a game of cards. The hand you are dealt is
determinism; the way you play it is free will."

– Jawaharlal Nehru

Points of Light

Gerry – *I find it amazingly hard to stop my brain from turning all the time. It never wants to stop. This is the first time I've ever really gotten the idea it should. I thought we were supposed to be thinking all the time. I understand why that isn't always true now, and I'm beginning to get some ideas about how to stop it – or at least slow it down. Every once in a while, I get a few moments where I am feeling or doing, but not really thinking. It's relaxing when it happens and kind of exciting to understand that I don't have to be gazing at a mountain vista or some other breathtaking thing to actually chill and be still.*

Loretta – *When it comes to emotions, I am a burier from way back. For as long as I can remember, I've pushed my feelings down inside and tried to pretend that I didn't have any feelings but good ones. I think it started when I was younger. There were so many people around me that were too emotional, that I tried to go in the opposite direction. My family had it all. There were siblings who thrived on emotional drama or ran from their feelings by being busy all the time. Mom hid her hurt with worry and dad was like me – he hid his. None of them were healthy although some of those approaches looked better on the surface. The idea that feelings and thoughts are different, is a new idea to me. Learning to feel my emotions is too. It's scary. I'm afraid there is so much emotion inside me that I won't be able to handle it. But I know I have too. I can't figure me out by bottling up one of the most important parts of me – my heart.*

Me – _____

_____

_____

_____

_____

_____

_____

_____

_____

Finding Our SoftSpot*

As a rule, One Percenters are more likely forced to traverse a
rock-strewn path up a hill than to naturally meander onto soft
grass on a sloping meadow. We are therefore compelled to work
twice as hard to find a softer place.

That outcome doesn't happen by accident, luck, fantasy, or
short-cuts. The best ways to stay ahead of a hard life usually
involve hard work.

On that journey, it's important to remember that we are striving
to reach for our best – not to simply be the best. A person with
severe developmental disabilities who learns to use a spoon
merits at least as much respect as a good athlete.

What we do for a living, who we spend time with, and other
external life choices will play a part in taking us to hard or soft
places. What we do inside ourselves will remain the ultimate
determinant of our success or failure.

All this means lots of work that's seldom partnered with quick
fixes. For most of us, it takes years to find our softspot. For
some of us, it takes a lifetime. . .

After the military came college. He discovered deeper abilities than he imagined. Academics were easy – the social, though, was as tough as ever.

He learned something else: education was a giant stepping stone. Once you had it, no one could take it away.

There was school and more school. Learning became somewhat of an addiction. He marveled at the difference in his interest in high school (it was for the system) and college (it was for him).

It took effort, but with education there was hope.

He landed on psychology by default. His original plan was to become a physician's assistant or something more, but he kept hitting timing and expense barriers. Besides, he liked learning about what made people, and himself, tick.

First, there was a psychology degree. Then, came a graduate education degree, followed by another in social work. He finished with a doctorate in psychology. Most of his time in school he worked on the side. Each day he studied helped solidify a clearer life map.

The stage of putting that education into practice was daunting. The skills necessary to working with emotional, social, personal, and family problems were endless. Earlier lessons on the "imposter syndrome" hit home. The challenges of helping were unyielding.

He knows now how he did it. Fear of failure haunted him, but it did not stop him. He felt drawn to grow toward some purpose he couldn't define or understand. He was compelled to stay with what was almost always a painful but productive walk.

Looking back, he found one underlying quality that made the crucial difference. His courage button was bigger than his fear button. He was thereby able to keep on going. . .

Thinking Things

In the mountains, June is one of the best months. Days are long, and nights are cool and quiet. It's when fireflies come out.

Since he'd been a little boy, he had always thought lightning bugs were magical. Catching them in jars filled with twigs, enjoying their light through the night, and turning them loose the next day was a cherished sequence of memories.

The sad thing was how quickly they died away as the summer wore on. Fireflies grew rare in July and were gone in August.

There was one notable exception. It was a moonless September night. At bedtime, he'd taken his birddog Pepper out for a break. While waiting on the deck, he happened to look up. There in the distance was a lone firefly coming his way.

He watched it. The seconds stretched as it crossed his field of view. The intensity of its light was exceptional. Its blinking was rapid and desperate. It was a stark exposure to aloneness.

Like a snowman in summer, this firefly was alive when it shouldn't have been. Its untimely flight silently declared, "I am still here!"

Those few seconds remain an imprinted memory. That solo flight of courage and determination serves as a reminder that "what is" does not always match our assumptions of "what should be."

Thoughts circled in his head long after the firefly had receded into the woods. He mentally searched for a landing place for what he had just witnessed. In that firefly's delayed search for connection was a message that will echo for a lifetime, "The darker the night, the brighter the light. . ."

Life is like a road bordered by two ditches.

Those ditches represent extremes.

Extremes breed more extremes – and if we are not careful, moving from ditch to ditch can become a life pattern.

Somewhere between extremes lies the road to reason.

We all travel further and better on that road.

A life well-lived must be aimed between the ditches.

"If you're in a ditch, and you're looking down, you can see where you're going but you can't see the way out."

– Jen Sincero

If you're a One percenter, you'll have challenges.

Sometimes, there will be some very tough challenges.

That stress can leave us feeling split in two.

That can be a temporary or a permanent state of mind.

The difference is determined by one thing:

Whether or not we use those challenges to learn, nurture, and manage our head, heart, hand, and spirit.

If we're not pulling those together, we're coming apart.

"And the day came when the risk to remain tight in a bud was more painful than the risk it took to blossom."

– Anais Nin

Dreams are not all they seem to be.

And they can teach us a lot about ourselves.

But dream analysis can be a bit tough. That's because at night our brain is operating without anyone in charge. It can go to crazy places.

One helpful method is to identify the dream's key theme.

A very common theme is powerlessness.

Our dream's theme can be a strange but helpful flag.

Dreams can point out a key life issue needing our attention.

"Dreams digest the meals that are our days."

– Astrid Alauda

It's not possible to be in two places

at the same time.

But we still try.

Being where we are seems simple, but it's not.

Our world is flooded with relentless tugging distractions.

Like most human activities, being where we are is a skill.

It takes discipline to push distractions out of our head.

Think of these external temptations as kidnappers.

They come not as friends, but to steal us away.

"Do not look for happiness outside yourself.
The awakened seek happiness inside."

– Peter Deunov

143

Everyone has an inner voice.

Not everyone has a good one.

Our inner voice can be negative, neutral, or positive.

Neutral is almost as bad as negative.

A positive inner voice does not come naturally.
Being raised by or around positive people helps.

Ultimately, we must train ourselves to appreciate ourselves.

*"Once you replace negative thoughts with positive ones,
you'll start having positive results."*

– Willie Nelson

Critics and antagonists are a fact of life.

They will follow us wherever we go.

Their mission: raise themselves up by pushing us down.

There are some better ways to weigh critical messages:

If the message has merit: embrace it.

If the message has mischief: ignore it.

If the message has malice: discard it.

The trick is to learn from critics without hating them.

"If you don't have enemies, you don't have character."

– Paul Newman

Feeling Things

In the ninth grade, he failed algebra and was thus condemned to summer school. It turned out to be a good thing.

The teacher was in summer relaxed mode and took a practical approach. She made sense where none of the equations or symbols had made sense before.

Importantly, he had a chance to make friends with a couple of kindred spirits. An indifference to or a missing aptitude for math was a shared bond.

Both were the sons of ministers, one of whom was of international renown. As a child of another preacher's wayward son, he understood their challenges.

One day, he snuck some gin into school that he had taken out of his father's bar. Out under a tree, he shared it with his fellow captives during their lunch break out.

From that moment on, thanks to a handy soda machine, a gin and 7-Up cocktail became a daily ritual. His partners in mischief would pilfer the spirit from their neighbors, while he watered down his father's gin to conceal his own incremental theft.

The anticipation of their lunch-time adventure got them through the morning, and the slight buzz of the gin and 7-Up eased the drag of the afternoon.

In the end, all three managed to make a "C." It was good enough.

To this day, the taste of gin, 7-Up, friendship, and shared mischief remains a warm and pleasant memory. . .

Complex people need big doses of four things.

We need support, structure, safety and stability.

Support helps us over hurdles.

Structure keeps us moving.

Safety gives us freedom.

Stability gives us strength.

Everyone needs this help sometimes.

Starting out, complex people need this help all the time.

"My number one goal is to love, support
and be there for my son."

– Farrah Fawcett

Some emotions are stickier than others.

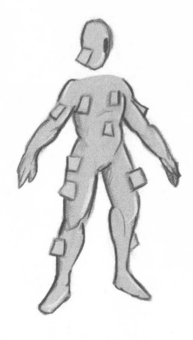

Emotions can grab hold and not want to let go.

Shame, anger, and fear are the stickiest of all.

And sticky quickly becomes stinky!

Peeling them off is an everyday mission.

"Shame isn't a quiet grey cloud, shame is a drowning man who claws his way on top of you, scratching and tearing your skin, pushing you under the surface."

– Kirsty Eagar

We all need human connection.

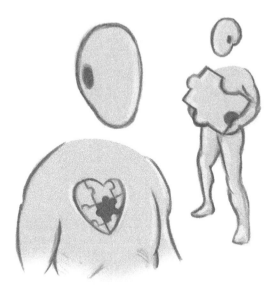

But it needs to be a good human connection.

Relationships based on dependency, habit, conflict, greed, manipulation, fear, anger, and control are not good.

A good relationship uplifts the participants.

It's our hearts – not scars – that we must rub together.

"Real connection and intimacy is like a meal, not a sugar fix."
– Kristin Armstrong

It's normal to try to escape painful feelings.

Many of us regularly use anger to that purpose.

That's a problem because emotions need direct attention.

Ever wonder why some people never grow up?

One reason – dodging deeper emotions chokes <u>all</u> growth.

Dealing with what we're really feeling does the opposite.

*"Anger, resentment and jealousy doesn't change
the heart of others – it only changes yours."*

– Shannon Alder

Feelings and thoughts often get entangled.

That's because they seem the same, but they are different.

Thoughts involve brain activity devoted to thinking.
Emotions involve heart activity devoted to feeling.

Like drinking and driving, when mixed, they're risky.

We have to learn to feel when we have feelings and think
when we have thoughts – but not at the same time.

Learning to feel versus think our way through emotions is
one of the most crucial and toughest of all life skills.

"The more you overthink the less you will understand."

– Habeeb Akande

Like everything in nature, people have seasons.

No one gets to be here forever.

Death's touch is stark, and it can come abruptly.

To never again be able to see, touch, hear, smell or experience a person is a staggering hurdle.

Grief for our loss in normal and necessary.

Some cry, some mourn, some anguish, and some get angry, but the best form of grief is growth.

That growth happens when we ask ourselves what those we have lost would want us to do, and then do it.

"Clouds come floating into my life, no longer to carry rain or usher storm, but to add color to my sunset sky."

– Rabindranath Tagore

The presence of fear can be a sign of success.

A life of comfort is not stressful; a life of growth is.

Examples: drugs, alcohol, porn, and video games = easy.
Facing challenges, doubts, and responsibilities = not easy.

Moving from the first to the latter magnifies fear.

This is a sign of progress that may seem like failure.

That's a big reason many people don't grow: it's scary.

No huffing and puffing = no productive action.

A stuck car just slings mud.

"Many times, the thought of fear itself is
greater than what it is we fear."

– Idowu Koyenikan

Pain is a crucial ingredient for development.

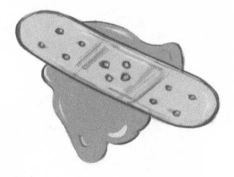

But suffering for suffering's sake is a mistake.

Pain is, above all, a teacher.

No one who ever accomplished anything did so without first walking through a meadow of pain.

Anxiety, for example, can be a garden for compassion.

It's so painful that it teaches us about the pain of others.

Thus, we all have an unavoidable mission.

Never submit to or argue with pain: listen, learn and grow.

"Out of suffering have emerged the strongest souls; the most massive characters are seared with scars."

– Kahlil Gibran

Doing Things

There were three words that stood out from his experience in Vietnam.

One was a four-letter profanity used by almost everyone there to spice up everything, everywhere. It took practice to retire that word when he came home. Embarrassment at allowing it to accidentally slip out at his mother's dinner table aided the transition. He came to understand there's a difference in a powerful word and a good one.

The second memorable word was "tired." Though the average age of the participants was nineteen, he and his peers always seemed to be complaining of exhaustion. Heat, uncertainty, fear, routine, urgency, and violence were a potent formula for weariness.

The third word was "lonely." No matter how much he and others tried to drink, joke, or otherwise push the lonesomeness away, it was almost always there. Being surrounded by people was not the same thing as being emotionally connected.

He found his best companion on a dusty merchant's table in a place called "Dog Patch" outside of Danang. It was, of all things, a German-made Hohner harmonica. That "C" key harp was new. He purchased it with no idea of how to use it.

He had never studied music, but he could whistle. Discarding the instructions, he started mentally searching for notes to "On Top of Old Smokey" and slowly taught himself.

With practice, he got pretty good at making that harmonica a friend that could play most anything. Neil Young's "The Needle and the Damage Done" still echoes. Out of effort came reward.

What stands out most now is how often that harmonica filled in the lonely moments. It was ready whenever he was. It still is. . .

Life is intended as an adventure.

In a hard world it's easier to tremble than to thrive.

Enduring life finds us treating our gifts like burdens, our blessings like curses, and our talents like intrusions.

It's not ours to question why we are what we are.

It's ours to step forward with gusto, and embrace and grow our gifts to their fullest potentials.

It's in the midst of uninsured moments we find our best.

"Life's either a daring adventure or nothing."

– Helen Keller

The word "yes" is a great trigger for action.

But without a "no" button, "yes" is dangerous.

We live in a society increasingly antagonistic to limits.
We want what we want when we want it.

Those suggesting restraint are viewed as naive.

But "no" is often a better friend than "yes."

Adults and kids need brakes as surely as gas pedals.

"No" also often takes more courage than "yes."
The two should only be purchased as a matched set.

"It takes true courage and real humility to say NO or YES!"

– E. Yeboah

In the modern world, we face a deceptively limited set of choices: spills, pills, or skills?

Every new day gives an opportunity to choose.

Our options are clear and they have clear impacts.

Stumble around in misery.

Take legal or illegal drugs to ease our symptoms.

Do battle with our hurdles through learned skills.

Nature's relentless message is "LEARN AND GROW!"

That means we really don't have a choice.

At least not a good one.

Learned skills are to humans what gas is to a car.

"He who moves not forward, goes backward."

– von Goethe

Each generation encounters new challenges.

And each passes on the good and the bad to their children.

The Greatest Generation faced survival, won, and then unknowingly taught their offspring to be selfish.

Baby boomers mistakenly marketed the fantasy that the world is a yet to be perfected form of Disneyland.

The children of the 21st century have thus inherited a learned temptation to wait for a magic ride.

No generation has ever been able to avoid the inevitabilities of personal responsibility.

In the end, all of us must learn, adjust, and press on.

"Parenthood – it's about guiding the next generation and forgiving the last."

– Peter Krause

Problems are everywhere.

That's why problem-solvers are so important.

There are three paths to responding to difficulties:

Avoid solving problems.
Solve problems through negative approaches.
Solve problems through positive approaches.

Anger, obstinacy, and violence are negative means.

Creativity, persistence, and fairness are positive means.

In a world with a growing list of problems, we need more
people operating out of positivity, maturity, and courage
than out of avoidance, criticism, and hostility.

"Problems are only opportunities in work clothes."

– Henry Kaiser

Stress comes in one of two forms – circular or linear.

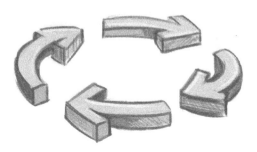

Linear stress has a beginning, a middle, and an end.

There are problems but also workable solutions.

An easy example: brushing to get rid of morning breath.

Circular stress has us going in circles.

There is no end and there are no easy solutions.

Bills that exceed our income are an example.

Linear stress is life. Circular stress is death.

There are answers.

Relentlessly cut and bend the circle 'til you find solutions.

"I'm trapped by my obsession, but I'm set free by my decisions."

– Anthony T. Hincks

The head, heart, hand, and spirit are a team.

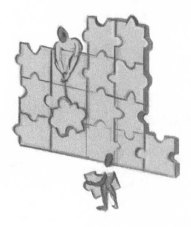

Like all teams, they require training to work together.
We usually have one strength seeking to rule the rest.
And it's commonly the one that comes easiest.

Allowing one part to kidnap the others is risky.

It's better for the others to keep the rogue in check.
Managing the team takes practice.

It starts with teaching the three to rule the one instead of
allowing the one to rule the three.

"Overthinking arises when you are disconnected - disconnected
from the body, mind, soul, society and the nature."

– Amit Ray

There are three armies we fight in life. . .

The past, the present, and the future.

We can fight one and win.
We can fight two and maybe win.
When we fight three – we always lose.
Complex people are prone to taking on all three.

The present is the foundation of the past and the future.

That's where we should concentrate.

It's called the "Precious Present" for many good reasons.

"Nothing is worth more than this day."

– von Goethe

It's sort of like we are all born in a pool. . .

. . .with a shallow and deep end.

Those in the shallow end can stand or swim easily.
Those in the deep end start out laying on the bottom.

It's lonely, scary and overwhelming down there.

You can see the laughter and fun of the shallow end.
But you don't know how to get there.

We all need help to learn how to swim in the deep end.

*"Loneliness and the feeling of being
unwanted is the most terrible poverty."*

– Mother Teresa

We can learn as much from losing as winning.

Winning is addictive, and if it is unchecked, it can spoil, distract, and corrupt us like all other addictions.

Losing is painful and thus less attractive. We can become familiar with losing, but we rarely are addicted to it.

Losing pushes us to look for a better way.

And looking for a better way is the father of progress.

Failure is vital to life, just like a shell is crucial to a nut.

"Success is not final. Failure is not fatal.
It is the courage to continue that counts."

— Winston Churchill

To be alive is to be in a race.

We can walk, sprint, or even crawl, but it's helpful to remember we are in a long-distance run.

A stumble here and there is to be expected, and the first and fastest is not always the winner.

The goal is to run the race, not prove anything to anyone.

To cross the line, we are mostly racing against ourselves.

"Life is a marathon, not a sprint."

– Ivanka Trump

Right Things

He had heard of people who experienced the voice of God. He envied that validation. His connection had always been a bit less direct. Looking back, he can now see that it takes a special kind of surrender for one to feel our higher authority as something real.

Man is forever cynical even about the things in front of him. It is not surprising that a creature who can thus deny the tangible acts of The Holocaust and 9-11 might have trouble embracing the ethereal.

In spite of the pain that life had always held, he never blamed God. In truth, he had always felt tangibly blessed by something bigger than himself. But with two notable exceptions, that relationship was always more thoughtful than personal.

One involved a patient with a seemingly insurmountable and potentially catastrophic problem for which he had no answers. Standing at his kitchen sink one morning he asked God for help, and to his surprise, the clear answer immediately popped into his head. It wasn't a delusion. It was help – specific, direct help.

The second episode was when he was running for public office. Between traveling seventeen counties, working full-time, and enduring the sliceable misery of running for office, he was desperately weary. He remembers praying for rest one night and immediately feeling a sense of peace as he fell into a deep sleep.

For the first time in a year, he woke without exhaustion. He knew he had experienced a very direct kind of grace affirming there was something more than just what he could see and touch. That experience strengthened his search for more. . .

People in pain naturally seek self-protection. . .

. . .for heart, mind, and spirit as surely as hand.

These defenses were once needed, but just as a fort can be a prison, defenses can become a barrier to growth.

Crabs outgrow their shells.

Letting go of defenses is like saying goodbye to an old friend who's no longer good for us.

It's a hard thing, but a good thing.

"It would be better to be deceived a hundred times than to live a life of suspicion."

– Charles Haddon Spurgeon

Progress in life is only rarely a big event.

It's mostly a result of little moments adding up.

Our life mission isn't moving mountains.

Moving shovel-loads of dirt moves those mountains.

Sometimes we believe we must leap toward greatness.

More surely, we touch heaven with a million small steps.

"The Devil is in the details, but so is salvation."

- Hyman G. Rickover

Every life is a private journey.

Like snowflakes, we fall inimitably through the same sky.

Though we may learn from others, we can't be like them.

Nor can we change how we're designed.

But we can expand to our fullest and brightest potentials.

Life's mission is to embrace who we are and get bigger.

*"Always remember that you are absolutely unique.
Just like everyone else."*

– Margaret Mead

There is a secret that no one tells us.

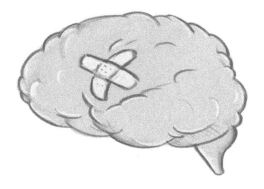

We all have a fatal flaw.

It may be damage, a limitation, a hindrance, or disability.
It may be visible or hidden, but it's <u>always</u> there.

It's God's way of keeping us humble, grounded, and
searching for something more.

Fatal flaws aren't necessarily fatal.

Yes, it's true that nobody is perfect.

But we can always improve.

Have no fear of perfection - you'll never reach it.

– Salvador Dali

Realizing we are a One percenter can be liberating.

It helps explain the unexplained and point to solutions.

But there are other things to remember-

1% measures our potential, not our outcome.

Ability without work is a container without content.

Complexity is a responsibility, not a prize.

It's important to understand that our gifts come with conditions, and that effort is the fifth element that takes it all from a burden to a blessing.

"Nothing in the world is worth having or worth doing unless it means effort, pain, difficulty... I have never in my life envied a human being who led an easy life. I have envied a great many people who led difficult lives and led them well."

– Theodore Roosevelt

An inner critical voice is aimed at abuse, not truth.

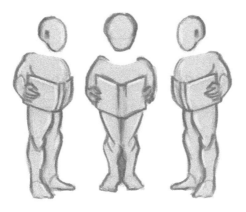

What it tells us rarely has anything to do with reality.

Mostly it's just a recycling of old hurts.

Over time, painful moments unite in a chorus singing a false and sour tune: "You're Unworthy!"

Ours should be the only voice in our head and it should be trained to be positive, responsible and supportive.

It begins with aggressively firing the chorus members.

That's a one-by-one sort of thing.

"Write injuries in sand, kindness in marble."

– Anonymous

Life – every life – has three phases.

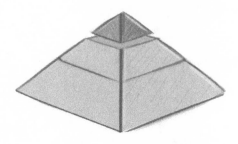

We may or may not participate in all of them.

The first is centered on our upbringing – everyone faces good and bad. Parenting nor childhood are ever perfect.

The second begins when we are on our own and start making our own choices – often as duplication or in opposition to how we were raised. Defenses take charge and form a protective shell.

The third is when we decide to quit living in reaction to our youth and become more maturely dedicated to positive values, opportunities and potentials.

Most people never get to Phase Three. They spend their lives reacting to the world through earlier trauma or harms.

The test is to press on and refuse to be defined by the past.

It's often said that a traumatic experience early in life marks a person forever, pulls her out of line, saying, "Stay there. Don't move."

– Jeffrey Eugenides

We may not reach our potential on society's schedule.

It can take years, decades, or even a lifetime to land.

Forget the expectations of others.

What they think or say doesn't matter.
What matters is what's true.

What is true?

We must never stop learning, growing, and searching for
our deeper purpose until our time is done.

And some don't reach their stride until late in the race.

"I was a shy kid, a late bloomer.
At 22, I was probably 16 emotionally."

– Chris Pine

We all spend time in troubled seas.

It takes more than one life jacket to keep us afloat.

Real "life" jackets come in many forms.

Work, family, exercise, hobbies, relationships, education, church, and volunteering are positive examples.

Unsupported lives are easily sunk by choppy moments.

The more we've got to hold us up, the less easily we'll sink.

But life jackets only work if we put them on.

"It's not so much how busy you are, but why you are busy. The bee is praised. The mosquito is swatted"

– Mary O'Connor

Generational age differences are mostly a myth.

The flavorings change, but the core ingredients don't.

All cars have a motor, tires, seats, and windows.

Styles and details change, but cars remain the same.

We are thus touched, not bound, by our age.

Each age has new trails to blaze in new ways.

"Old words are reborn with new faces."

— Criss Jami

No matter the ailment, hurdle, or puzzle, L-O-V-E is the world's best medicine.

It helps all of us to glue our pieces together.

Love comes in two doses.
The love we give and the love we get.
Both count, but the first has the deepest impact.

For those seeking instruction, pets can point the way.

Dogs teach us how to be loved. Cats teach us how to love.

Loving and being loved are skills requiring daily practice.

*"If we could read the mind of animals,
we would find only truths."*

– Anthony Douglas Williams

All humans seek the respect of those we respect.

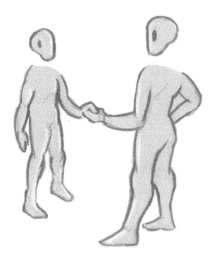

But respect must be built.

We are all stuck with the reality that no matter how tough our hurdles, we have to keep trying.

We are never ever able to simply give in or give up.

That's a foundation for the deepest kind of respect.

And one more thing, respect is earned – never given.

"Make improvements, not excuses. Seek respect, not attention."

– R. Bennett

There's growing misery in the world.

Much of it perpetrated by miserable people.

They are best identified by four traits – a tendency toward anger, control, drama, and negativity.

All four are addictive. All four are a powerful but hollow source of personal identity. All four are toxic.

What can we do in response to such miserable people?

It begins with simply refusing to become like them.

"Oftentimes, when people are miserable, they will want to make other people miserable, too. But it never helps."

– Lemony Snicket

There are three kinds of people in the world.

Those who make, those who break, and those who take.

Takers search for something in exchange for nothing.
Breakers find distraction in destroying vs. creating.
Makers find fulfillment in adding to the world.

The first is captured by the anger found in dependency.
The second knows the transient joy of a dumpster burner.
It is only in the third one that one finds sustainable cheer.

Nature rewards those who keep the planet turning, and
assures unlimited opportunities for our participation.

"Be the one who nurtures and builds.
Leave people better than you found them."

— Marvin J. Ashton

Gifts can turn to darkness as surely as light.

Complex people can be very good at being bad.

It's like a candle.

Held upright, it is a source of light and warmth.

Knocked over, it becomes a source of danger.

We are all pulled in both directions.

The greater our potential, the more we will be pulled.

Never yield. Always learn, reset, and press on.

"It was important, Dumbledore said, to fight, and fight again, and keep fighting, for only then could evil be kept at bay, though never quite eradicated..."

– J.K. Rowling

On our arrival, we get a bucket of happy spots.

Their number is limited, so they must be used with care.

There are a million ways to steal from our bucket –
including addictions, bad choices, and shortcuts.

The good news is that our bucket can be refilled.
A guy named Solomon showed us the value found in the
"4-L's" of laboring, learning, loving, and living.

In these four activities, we find replenishment.

Stealing is easy and fast – replenishing is slow and hard.

The best plan is to avoid robbing our own bucket.

"All happiness depends on courage and work."

– Honoré de Balzac

A good filter for what matters and doesn't is vital.

Try a simple 'one, two, three' approach.

Priority One: Following our core values

Priority Two: Embracing our day to day responsibilities

Priority Three: Skipping life's chatter and clutter

The first lead the way and land in peace. We must face the second, but then lay them down. The last aren't worth picking up to begin with.

Where we put our energy must be a conscious choice.

Constant turmoil means we're missing something.

Sometimes it means we're ignoring a One, overthinking a Two, or failing to lay down a Three and thus giving into our mind's relentless craving for chatter and clutter.

"Trust in the LORD and do good; dwell in the land and enjoy safe pasture."

– Psalm 37:3

**The gift of life rarely follows a happily
ever after script.**

Everything will involve a mix of good and not so good.

This is especially true when something involves people.

All relationships command patience and realism.

It's all part of nature's plan.

The same tree that provides you with cooling shade in the
summer will dump leaves on your lawn in the fall.

"You have to take the good with the bad."

– American proverb

We are all teachers.

To live is to be a model, a tutor, and an influence to others.

We have that responsibility whether we want it or not.

Our only choice is how well we take up the charge.

Harsh approaches to teaching and coaching can work.

But isn't there already enough of that in a harsh world?

Grace, wisdom, a push, and a wink are the best teachers.

"The mediocre teacher tells. The good teacher explains. The superior teacher demonstrates. The great teacher inspires."

– William Arthur Ward

No one has all the answers.

No one needs all the answers.

Life is a continual process of learning.

Expecting too much, too quickly, leads to shortcuts. . .

Life is like paddling a deep river versus running rapids.

We have a long way to go.
And we need patience to get there.

"The only things worth learning are the
things you learn after you know it all."

- Harry S. Truman

Life reliably presents us all with a simple decision.

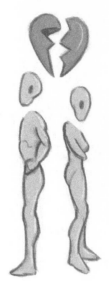

We can be true to our heart and nature.

We can be true to our scars and defenses.

Whichever we practice will set our course.

Our course, in turn, will determine our destination.

Which path is more likely to end in a better place?

"All defensiveness and emotional tumult is a fear response because of your need for acceptance and ruthless control of the territory of your safe fantasy world."

– Bryant McGill

A liberated spirit needs a safe landing field.

In a deceptive world, finding one is harder than it seems.

Here are some things to look for:

Dedicated to spiritual or earthly power?

Comes from the grace of God or the hands of man?

Unleashes through love or traps in hate?

Steadfast to deeper truths or dogma?

Presses for growth or impairs through comfort?

Tested by time or "new and improved?"

More about faith or ritual and religiosity?

Liberates with duty or unleashes with laxity?

Reaches and teaches or prosecutes and persecutes?

Stands as a compass or flows with the wind?

It's popular to scorn the value of spiritual faith.

Yet everywhere lies evidence of something more.

And people of faith do better than those without.

"Fear is faith in reverse."

– Zig Ziglar

Points of Light

Diane – *I like the idea of looking at myself from four different directions. I've always viewed me as sort of like a bowl of soup with everything mixed together. Separating myself into different pieces makes it easier to understand and work on the things I need to work on. Before, it was like trying to pick celery out of my soup. I don't like celery, but it's not easy to locate and remove when it's mixed in with all the other stuff. I continue to have a hard time separating my feelings from my thoughts. They sometimes seem like one and the same. But I understand that what works for the head doesn't necessarily work for the heart and vice versa. Trying to work on me remains a daily challenge, but at least I now understand I do not have a choice. Before I was sort of waiting for the real me to bloom or some big outside event to come along and rescue me from my misery.*

Jake – *I've never given much thought to my spiritual side. I've toyed with different notions about a higher power, but most of the time that was more about entertainment than a sincere search for answers. Growing up, there was hardly anyone in my family who went to church or otherwise participated in religious activities. My friends blew religion off pretty much as old-people superstition, and I more or less thought like they did. Occasionally, though, I did have exposure to someone who had an interest in faith and lived it. Those rare people seemed to have something I didn't, and so at some point, I did at least start paying more attention in my search for religious people who seemed genuine. In reading this book I was a little surprised to see that one's spirituality was held in equal measure to one's head, heart, and hand. It makes sense, but it's never anything I've really considered.*

Me – _____
_____
_____
_____
_____
_____
_____
_____

CHAPTER ELEVEN

Do's and Don'ts

* Do [v. dü] To bring to pass; carry out...

Every day we all face relentless pressures to make choices about what we should and should not do. Some of those choices are clear and effortless. Some – and often it feels like most – hold stark uncertainty.

Personal choice holds an astonishing capacity to uplift or impair. It is thus a gift of unparalleled importance that should be embraced with care.

Over the course of our life, what we choose to do or not to do leaves lasting marks. That impact – good as surely as bad – also inevitably carries over to others.

Here are a few "do's and don'ts" which have special applications for complex people attempting to navigate through a challenging world. . .

The decision to have children were two of his best. In both cases, that choice was more attached to his recognition of a mother's need than his own. It was a wise choice, for like all children, they were special.

His first child came early. Very early and she had to spend a good bit of time in prenatal care. It made a difference. She was precious from the start, but he still had to work on learning how to love her. It wasn't as natural as he had assumed. He found that the more he invested in her care, including the baths, diapers, and middle-of-the-night stuff, the more their bond grew. It didn't take long.

She was around two when he separated from her mother. The memory of his daughter in that crib saying, "Mommy and Daddy are not going to live together anymore, and I've got to be strong," still echoes all these years later. It was a hard way to begin a new life. Her young heart needed him to be more careful.

The second child, a son, was both easier and harder. He was a boy, and because he was a boy, he was more frightening than his sister. The fear of doing to his son what his father had done to him was unconsciously strong. He didn't want to damage his son with the same anger, criticism, and detachment.

Looking back, he did more right than wrong with his kids. Excepting his mistakes with their mothers, he intentionally worked to be a good dad. Most of the time he stepped over his own pain to make them feel loved. It matters that he did better by his children than was done to him.

It wasn't all they deserved, but it was enough to give them a fair start. They were a very important reason to keep on going. . .

We <u>do</u> get to feel and experience anger.

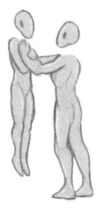

We don't get to feed it by acting out or storing it.

Ventilated anger is more often renewed than relieved.

Throwing it about does exactly the same thing.
Holding on to anger allows it to fester.

Looking for offenses helps it grow.

The clincher: Feeding anger also feeds depression.

Solutions?

Embrace the antidotes: reason, love, and forgiveness.

"How much more grievous are the
consequences of anger than the causes of it."

– Marcus Aurelius

We <u>do</u> get to consider our own needs.

We don't get to be the center of the universe.
Self-absorption is an addictive temptation.

That's especially true for people in pain.
Think of self-fascination as a recreational drug.

The high is very short-lived.

Human beings are designed like flashlights.
We are meant to shine outward, not inward.

*"In an individual, selfishness uglifies the soul; for the human
species, selfishness is extinction."*

– David Mitchel

We <u>do</u> get to feel sorrow for ourselves.

We don't get to make self-pity a lifestyle.

In a hard world, occasional weariness is normal.

We can feel sorry for ourselves just like we can for others.

But that's a place to visit and catch our breath.
Not a place to sit down and set up camp.

We're left with a simple life fact.

The only way out of the hardspots is to keep moving.

"All depression has its roots in self pity, and all self pity is rooted
in people taking themselves too seriously."

– Tom Robbins

We <u>do</u> deserve grace and mercy for our mistakes.

We don't get a pass on liability for those mistakes.

Accountability is important.

Without it, there's no spur to avoid echoing our errors.

Mistakes are normal and can be productive.

But only if we learn, forgive, and move forward.

Relentless self-punishment teaches us nothing.

But a failure to learn is an even greater mistake.

*"Anyone who has never made a mistake
has never tried anything new."*

– Albert Einstein

We <u>do</u> need a timeout from life's challenges.

We don't always get them in the way we wish.

It's like being in the game versus sitting on the bench.
Life was meant to be played, not observed.

Rest and recovery matter, but activity matters more.

Too much intensity burns us out.
Too little leads to stagnancy.

There's a good place in the middle.

*"If every time we fall short of our aspirations, we lower them, it
won't take long before we plummet to sloth."*

– Joe Beaton

We d<u>o</u> get a normal measure of worry and rest.

We don't get to worry near as much as we get to sleep.

Sleep helps us reset and refresh.
Too much and we miss out on life.
Too little does the same thing.

Thinking helps us face and respond to life.
Too much thinking and we also miss out on life.
Too little thinking and we run into the obstacles in life.

With thinking, the goal is to find a point of balance.
Unlike sleeping, it's a skill that takes lots of practice.

"When action grows unprofitable, gather information; when information grows unprofitable, sleep."

– Ursula K. LeGuin

We <u>do</u> get to sometimes doubt the value of life.

We don't get to act on that discouragement.

Occasional thoughts on leaving it all behind are normal.

Turning that temptation into action is not.

Not only do we surrender the gift of life,

we also crush the people around us.

The phrase, "no one will miss me" doesn't work.

How can we ever be sure?

We can never know who might need us in the future.

"But in the end one needs more courage
to live than to kill himself."

– Albert Camus

We <u>do</u> get to have many special moments in life.

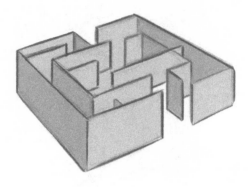

We don't get to skip our share of stressful challenges.

We are rarely in direct charge of our stressors.
But we do get to pick how we handle them.
A stress-free place, job, or time is a myth.

It exists only in fairytales.

There's a reason: without stress, we don't grow.

Without growth, we can't survive.

*"It's not the load that breaks you down,
it's the way you carry it."*

– Lou Holtz

We <u>do</u> have the freedom to lead a simple life.

We don't necessarily get to be content with such.

A complex world yields complex problems.
Complex people are needed to solve those problems.

Those with extra gifts rarely get to wear just one hat.
That's challenging, but it's okay.

Life is richer with variety and responsibility.

"Liberty means responsibility. That is why most men dread it."
– George Bernard Shaw

We <u>do</u> get to apply our strengths as we wish.

We don't have permission to ignore those strengths.

Think of a canoe and a paddle.
One is nothing without the other.

Our head, heart, hand, and spirit are a team.
They must work together.
Neglect one, and the others are affected.

We have to exercise our gifts to keep them.

"Sacrifice is a part of life. It's supposed to be. It's not something to regret. It's something to aspire to."

– Mitch Albom

Points of Light

Jose – *My emotional processor is broken for sure. I can tell from any number of things. My emotions go from being frozen or lost to spewing all over the place. I can feel one thing one minute and something totally the opposite a few moments later. My highs are sometimes too high and my lows are definitely really low. I'm not clear how to fix it, but it makes sense that I've got to be the one working hardest to figure out how to fix it. I don't guess I should be surprised. My Dad bottled up his emotions, and now that I looked back, so did my mom. Dad's big emotion was anger and mom's was crying. They didn't know any more about dealing with emotions that I do now. It wasn't that they didn't have them, they just didn't know what to do with them. Sounds like me. I've got a chance to do something about this flaw. It's caused me too many problems for too long.*

Angie – *I'm a technology addict. I like my screens and they like me. There is relief in getting lost in my phone or computer that I don't get the same way anywhere else. I understand the pixel-addiction thing, but honestly I think it's better than a lot of other addictions. Even as I say that though, I can feel it's still wrong. I've noticed that a lot of my screen time just has me going in circles. My mind and fingers are occupied, but I can feel that I'm being drained by the experience. It's like that thing you said earlier, addiction, apparently to anything, stops us from growing while we are practicing the addiction. I may learn things on my screens, but it does seem to stunt my growth. I don't need that. Who does?*

Me – _____
_____
_____
_____
_____
_____
_____
_____
_____
_____

CHAPTER TWELVE

The Power

* Power [n. pou€r] The ability to do something or act in a
particular way, especially as a faculty for quality...

The journey from gift to burden to blessing is never on an easygoing or seamless course. Success is more surely measured by perseverance than an absence of errors or a parade of successes.

Still, like all first-class endeavors, the journey is special unto itself. For those who press forward, there is a tangible bonus. Somewhere, somehow, at some point, we work our way to our place in the world.

That is, after all, a major reason we are tasked with heavier hurdles. It's never about being superior so much as being different and tested on a unique path to becoming useful.

Those with the courage, character, and conviction to press on will discover a power that's out of the ordinary, humble, and worthy.

In a tricky world, that's a nifty landing. . .

Politics was the worst of it. There was a sense of vulnerability that, even with experience, never seemed to fade. It had something to do with the fact that those who voted against you were usually critical, and those who voted for you frequently felt you owed them something.

The toughest part was sticking to promises and principles. Once elected, everything about the political world seemed dedicated to extinguishing those priorities.

Though the opposite seemed true for most politicians, his moments of confidence were few. When so many were selling the promise of something for nothing, sticking with what seemed right was a lonely path that didn't lend itself to certainty.

Public service was hurtful, and he never developed a thick skin. Well-intended voices were constantly pushing him to do so as a means of hardening himself against the "dirty world of politics."

Today, it is a personal satisfaction that he held faith in keeping his heart open, unprotected, and thus vulnerable. Even with the relentless pressure, he knew that a thick skin leads to a thick head.

There was one very special thing that came from spending two decades in political arenas – he grew. It was never really fun and he was never comfortable, but he gained skills, knowledge, and strength he would have never learned in a comfortable place.

Time and experience taught him that, above all things, there is no earthly achievement more valuable than growth. He didn't always succeed in moving forward, but he did always learn and grow.

That evolution in knowledge, clarity, and priority made it worthwhile, and it helped him keep on going. . .

One Percenters have an edge.

We're made for the long run.

We start slow and get stronger with time.

That's good because life is less a sprint than a marathon.

But there is a catch.

First, we must embrace the challenge of the race.

"In general, any form of exercise, if pursued continuously, will help train us in perseverance.'

– Mao Zedong

One Percenters can see more – much more.

It has to do with having more than two eyes.

A strong head, heart, hand, and spirit can also see.
Using all four blesses us with remarkable vision.

We are rewarded with a 360-degree view.
Everyone gets to see unique, beautiful things.

Those climbing higher see more of those things.

"All men dream: but not equally. Those who dream by night in the dusty recesses of their minds wake up in the day to find it was vanity, but the dreamers of the day are dangerous men, for they may act their dreams with open eyes, to make it possible."

– T.E. Lawrence

One Percenters have extraordinary potential!

But potential has little value unless it's brought to life.

Mastering our complexities is a crucial key to that mission.

The head is the source of intelligence.
The head and the heart are the sources of wisdom.
The head, heart and hand are the sources of illumination.

But it takes the three and the spirit to gain enlightenment..

Embracing our complexity unleashes our fullest potential.

*"The road to enlightenment is long and difficult, and you should
try not to forget snacks and magazines."*

– Anne Lamot

One Percenters are often people of great impact.

That talent for success is a responsibility, not a prize.

Good things come harder than bad things.

Complex things are more difficult than simple things.

Pulling complex and good together is the hardest of things.

When we do, great moments appear on our horizon.

But that's only part of what it's all about.

We're here to make the planet better too.

"The enlightened are servants of the rich and poor, helpers of the weak and powerful, friends of the lowly and eminent. They are servants of mankind."

– Matshona Dhliwayoa

One Percenters civilize the world.

There are many ways we make our world a better place.

Our culture desperately needs positive inspiring role models. Complex people can be exceptional examples.

We live in a world filled with powers dedicated to hate, hinderance, and harm. The strength to stand for good is most surely found amidst the mastered complexities of a united head, heart, hand, and spirit.

Love is the greatest of gifts. It's enduring touch is found and magnified in a strong head, heart, hand, and spirit.

It takes a complex person to inspire, stand, and love.

"I actually think that the most efficacious way of making a difference is to lead by example, and doing random acts of kindness is setting a very good example of how to behave in the world."

– Misha Collins

One Percenters are liberated.

In a fallen world, only evil knows no bounds.

The rest of us always find obstacles to being free.

It takes great courage to be a truly free person.

It also takes a stout head, heart, hand, and spirit.

Slipping free from the restraints of "ordinary" is like
defying gravity – it's an action that demands a strong effort.

Thankfully, some of us are just not meant to stay put.

"I'd rather be interesting, original, and unique then follow the
pack. Revel in who you truly are and be liberated!"

– Amy Leigh Mercree

One Percenters are extraordinary problem solvers.

Confusing complexity is not far from powerful possibility.

That's good.

We're called on to uplift a world where problem-causers and problem-ignorers outnumber problem-fixers.

There are three truths that keep things in proper balance.

Those who create problems choke on their debris.

Ignoring problems only delays problems.

Problems solved last longer than problems created.

Fixing, building, helping, and creating are charitable.

Those who make the world better are the best of us.

"Think outside the square. Think for yourself don't just follow the herd. Think multidisciplinary!"

– Lucas Remmerswaal

One Percenters can be dynamos of courage.

That's because we go forward well-armed.

Strength of the head, heart, hand, and spirit is powerful.

It's not about vanity.

It has to become about valor.

Being better than others is a limited achievement.

Being stronger than fear is an extraordinary achievement.

Nothing good happens without bravery.

*"Success is not final; failure is not fatal:
it is the courage to continue that counts."*

– Winston S. Churchill

One Percenters are fortresses of conviction.

We stand for something, especially when facing hardship.

We are like sailors caught in a fog.
Our destination, not security, governs our course.

In today's world, most convictions are crafted for comfort.
Values are often less about principle than convenience.

Reaching for real conviction often means sacrificing both.

*"The relationship between commitment and doubt is by no means
an antagonistic one. Commitment is healthiest when it is not
without doubt, but in spite of doubt."*

– Rollo May

One Percenters delight in the gift of life.

Life is meant to be a joyful journey, not a trail of woe.

We are here to learn, grow, do, love, and enjoy.

The world is too absurd to treat it too seriously.

And there's enough misery without us adding to the mix.

The task is to be responsible, never too serious –
ever joyful.

Aim to leave behind love, memories,
and a playful footprint.

"I don't think of all the misery,
but of the beauty that still remains."

– Anne Frank

Points of Light

Joan – *I've spent my whole life feeling like I wasn't good enough. Part of it came from family members and others who seemed to need to make me feel that way. I helped them and even took over for them by becoming my own main source of criticism. I am sick of it. Thanks for teaching me there are other possibilities and that being different is not the same thing as being bad. I like that I am different and complex. I really am, and the idea that this is not really a limitation unless I make it so is exciting! That "You're not good enough" voice is very powerful, but it's been in my head too long. I'm going to defeat it. Thanks, one more time, for giving me an understanding of how it got started and why that voice is a liar I no longer have to listen to. It helps to feel like someone understands and, in a way, has my back.*

Gaby – *I like things to be simple. I especially like the clarity that there are things that work and things that don't, things that are good and things that are not, things that are right and things that are not. I like the values this book teaches, and I appreciate the way those values are presented. I felt like I was free to receive them or not. But honestly, I found most of them made sense and seemed right – even those that were new for me. There was a lot of information in this book. It helped that it was condensed into pages that were clear and concise. The words, the pictures, and the quotes helped make the point in a way I could understand. I had to think just enough to stay engaged, but not so much that I got lost. That's easy to do with too many words, and it's one of the reasons I avoid reading. There was a final thing I found helpful. Woven into most of the pages was a gentle call for action. From my own life experience, I know that unless I work on things, not much changes in my life. Thanks for reminding me of that in a soft way.*

Me – _____
_____
_____
_____
_____
_____

CHAPTER THIRTEEN

The Landing

* Land [v. land] To cause to reach or come to rest in a
particular place...

In the end, it all comes down to a few things. None of them are easy, but for those willing to stretch, neither are they out of reach.

For most of us, success and mastery will be a process – perhaps a long one. The complexity is in us, not in what we must do. Mastering our own urges, emotions, and other internal challenges is the toughest part of any growth equation.

But there is good news, really good news. Though we have very little control over life, we have measurable, meaningful control over ourselves.

First, we must decide we can't regulate this crazy world, what it thinks of us, or does to us. Then we can begin to better manage how we respond to whatever the world hands us.

That's when life gets extraordinary. . .

He continued to gain traction, but now it was more as a volunteer. He found he liked learning and growing almost as much as the one thing he came to know as the most important thing – loving others.

His work was demanding. He was his own boss, and yet he worked harder than most people with a real boss. He spent his days with people in pain, but he understood the opportunity to help them find their way to a better place was something to value versus endure. All those years of trial, error, and persistency began to pay off.

Looking back, he was especially grateful for the people who had been a softspot of encouragement, knowledge, and experience. Then there were the unpleasant people who unbeknownst to him sometimes became the best teachers.

Early on, he had figured out that hitting his stride was going to take a long time. He recognized that he had to keep his body alive long enough for his head, heart, hand, and spirit to catch up. Now, all that intentional effort spent taking care of himself was rewarded.

He was raised as a Christian, and though he never abandoned those values, he was sometimes careless with them. Along the way, he began to see something: The things he had been taught by prayer, the Bible, and the touch of the spiritually sincere were doggedly affirmed by the real world. Instead of finding it all to be a fantasy, he was continually surprised by the affirmed deeper truths of his earlier teachings. He celebrates that reunion every day.

So, what was life all about? Why all the hardships, hurts, and hurdles? He still wasn't sure, but his sense of joy accelerated.

The days still took work. Old fears, uncertainty, and confusion continued to gnaw on his door, but it was harder and harder for them to make it inside. He wanted more than ever to keep on going.

And so, in the end,
we find a few simple,
unrelenting, and
irreplaceable truths.

Never, never give up.

Take care of the box
you come in.

Be fully where you are. Live mostly in the moment and only a little in the past or future.

Look for good
role models.

Be one.

Grow your head,
heart, hand, and spirit
a little every day.

Get good at
something useful.
Don't stop doing it
until you replace it
with something as
good or better.

Forgive everyone,
every day, every time
– most especially
yourself.

Relentlessly reach for God's will and grace. Learn that the rules are laced with love, and that they are there for your benefit.

Pursue the truth and
the productive and
the positive, in all
things, and at
all times.